NORTH AMERICA
Country Studies

Reproducible

**Maps,
Facts,
Histories &
Questions**

Written By
RANDY L. WOMACK, M.Ed.
Learning Disabilities & Behavior Disorders
Illustrated By
CHRISTINA "Chris" LEW

Cover Design: **WOMACK & LEW**

A **Golden educational center publication**

P.O. Box 12
Bothell, WA 98041-0012

To Teachers and Parents

This book, <u>North America</u>, was written as a simplified, yet complete, resource book for you to use. The activities can be used as a supplemental resource for your regular history, social studies and/or geography curriculum. It is also a great overview to use when teaching Spanish as a foreign language.

There are fifteen separate sections in this book. The first fourteen sections are about the larger independent countries in North America. Each of the countries has a large 8 1/2 x 11" map, a one page current fact/information sheet (1990 Almanac), a short one or two page history through independence and one page of review questions. The last section is an answer key for the review questions.

New vocabulary words are introduced at the beginning of each section. If your students are capable of looking up the words in a dictionary, please have them do so. You might even have them use the words in their own sentences. It is suggested that you, as the teacher, go over the words with your students <u>before</u> the lessons are actually begun, making sure that the meanings are understood by the children. This will help your students grasp the concepts being taught.

The following page, "Important Information" can be given to your students to read. We think it is important to teach students why historical events took place and what the people were doing. It seems to help make the events more important to them. We hope you can elaborate on our brief discussions.

If you are interested in studying the countries of South America in the same easy-to-read format as this book, contact your local retail outlet for our book, **South America Country Studies**. If your retail outlet does not carry the book, contact Golden Educational Center to receive ordering information.

gOldEN EducatioNal CENTER
P.O. Box 12 • Bothell, Washington, 98041
(206) 481-1395

Copyright © 1991 *Golden Educational Center*
All rights reserved - Printed in U.S.A.
Published by Golden Educational Center
P.O. Box 12
Bothell, Washington 98041-0012

EXTRA INFORMATION

One reason that today's large cities are near the water is that they grew from early settlements. The people settled near major bodies of water, like the ocean, and large river outlets because that is where they first landed. Ships and boats were also their primary transportation for hundreds of years. The settlers also needed fresh water in order to live, so early settlers began living near rivers and lakes.

It is important to keep in mind that during the European exploration era, the main purpose of the European countries was to accumulate wealth and riches for their own countries. The rulers of the European countries cared very little about the people who were already living in the land to which they were sending exploration parties and soldiers.

In order for the wealth and riches to continue to flow to the respective European country, it was necessary for the goverments to send their own people over to set up trade stations and plantations. This was especially necessary for products that were not grown in Europe, such as sugar, tobacco, coffee and cotton.

The European settlers who came to the New World would just take the land and homes of the people already living in the area. They took the land without paying anything for it. They would often treat the people living in the area very harshly. Many times the people were made slaves so the merchants and plantation owners would not have to pay for the labor needed to do the hard work.

Soldiers were sent by the European leaders to maintain order and defeat any people who caused trouble or would fight back against the Europeans trying to take their land. The people in the New World would often fight back and try to gain their independence from the European rulers. They eventually gained their independence.

Gaining independence was hardly ever easy. It almost always took several years and thousands of people dying in the fighting. However, most of the people felt that freedom from the oppression of the European rulers was worth the cost.

While you read the short histories about the countries and people in this book, please keep in mind that people make history, not facts, dates or even the events themselves. Historical events are a result of people's individual and social attitudes, beliefs and practices. Only when people change their attitudes and beliefs will a history be written without such atrocities as mass murder, slavery, and other inhumane treatment of people.

It is my hope that you learn something from this book so you can be part of a future history book that will tell how people were respected, and even admired, for their individual differences.

Randy L.. Womack
Author

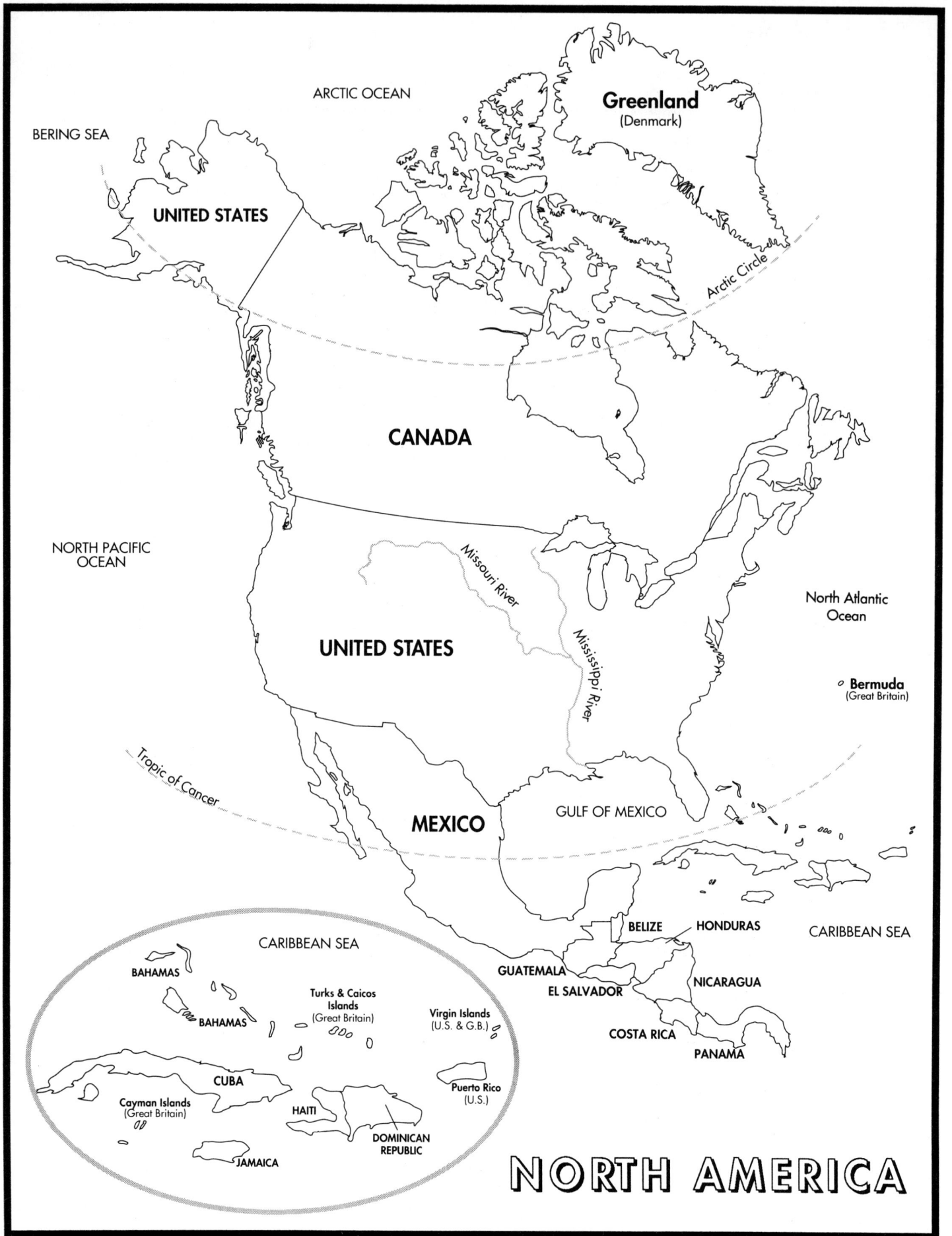

NORTH AMERICA

ARCTIC OCEAN

BERING SEA

Greenland
(Denmark)

UNITED STATES

Arctic Circle

CANADA

NORTH PACIFIC
OCEAN

Missouri River

Mississippi River

North Atlantic
Ocean

UNITED STATES

∘ **Bermuda**
(Great Britain)

Tropic of Cancer

MEXICO

GULF OF MEXICO

CARIBBEAN SEA

BELIZE   HONDURAS

GUATEMALA

EL SALVADOR

NICARAGUA

COSTA RICA

PANAMA

CARIBBEAN SEA

BAHAMAS

Turks & Caicos
Islands
(Great Britain)

Virgin Islands
(U.S. & G.B.)

BAHAMAS

CUBA

Cayman Islands
(Great Britain)

HAITI

Puerto Rico
(U.S.)

**DOMINICAN
REPUBLIC**

JAMAICA

NORTH AMERICA

NORTH AMERICA

North America
Section Contents

Bahamas

MAP • FACTS • HISTORY and REVIEW QUESTIONS

New Words to Learn:

Find the words in a dictionary and write the meanings on the line.

1. **abolished** - _____

2. **colony** - _____

3. **confederate** - _____

4. **enslave** - _____

5. **islets** - _____

6. **loyalist** - _____

7. **monarchy** - _____

8. **plantation** - _____

9. **treaty** - _____

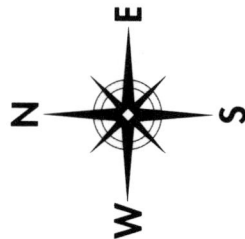

BAHAMAS

N E S W

BAHAMAS
(buh-HAH-muzh)

DATE of INDEPENDENCE: July 10, 1973, from England.

NATION'S CAPITAL CITY: Nassau.

OFFICIAL LANGUAGE: English.

FORM of GOVERNMENT: Constitutional **Monarchy**.

AREA: 5,380 square miles   (13,934 square kilometers).

POPULATION (est.1988): 242,983 people.   _Density_: 45 people per square mile.
17 people per square kilometer.
58% urban (city) living and 42% rural (country) living.

LARGEST CITY: Nassau - 139,000 people. Ranks 2nd largest in North America.

ELEVATION: _Highest_ - 206 feet (63 m) on Cat Island.
Lowest: sea level.

ADDITIONAL INFORMATION: About 700 islands and 2,300 **islets** make up the West
Indies independent nation of the Bahamas. Only about 20% of the Bahamas are
inhabited. • About two-thirds of the entire population live on only two islands.
Blacks make up about four-fifths of the population. The rest of the population is
mainly made up of whites or people of mixed white and black blood lines. • Today,
tourism brings in more money to the Bahamas than any other economic activity.

Bahamas' Flag

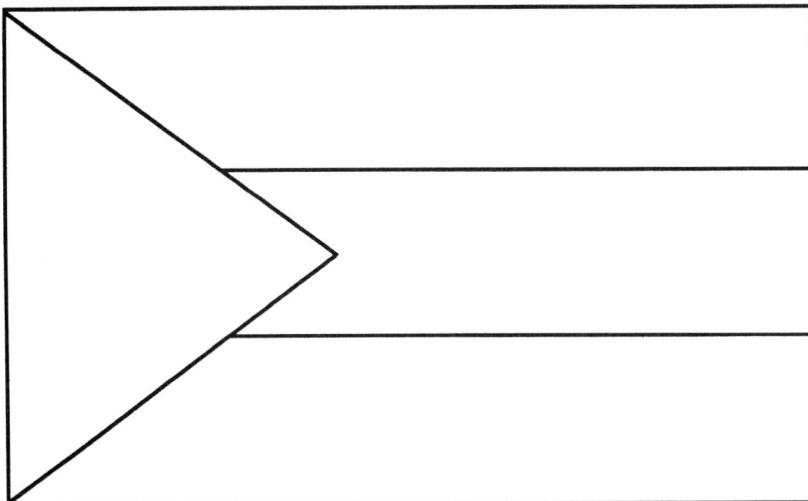

Flag Description

1. The top and bottom stripes of the flag are blue, while the center stripe is gold. The blue stripes stand for the sea and the gold stripe stands for the land.

2. The triangle on the left is black and symbolizes the people.

3. Color the flag the correct colors.

BAHAMAS

(buh-HAH-muz)

Name _____

Date _____

EARLY HISTORY in BRIEF

The Lucayo Indians were the first people to live in what is now the Bahamas. Christopher Columbus landed at San Salvador Island in 1492, and claimed it for Spain. The Spanish never settled in the Bahamas. However, they **enslaved** the Lucayo Indians and took many of them to do the heavy work in gold mines located on the islands of Cuba and Hispaniola. The British began settling in the Bahamas in the mid-1600's. Until then, very few people other than the native Indians lived on the islands.

At first, Spain seemed not to care that the British were settling in the Bahamas. However, in the late 1600's Spanish soldiers attacked many of the British settlements. The British settlements were also attacked by pirates who used the Bahamas as a base.

In 1717, the Bahamas became a British **colony**. The colonial government fought the pirates off after several years. Spain gave up all of its claims to the area in 1783, under the *Treaty of Versailles*.

After the Revolutionary War in America (United States 1775-1783), many British **Loyalists** came from the United States and settled in the Bahamas. These people brought their slaves and established **plantations** in the country. Britain **abolished** slavery in the Bahamas in 1838.

During the American Civil War (United States 1861-1865), the Bahamas were used as bases for **Confederate** and European trading ships. The islands were very prosperous during this time. After the war, the Bahamas had a decline in their economy. This went on until the mid-1900's when large numbers of tourists began to visit the islands.

Britain gave the Bahamas the right to rule itself in 1964.

❏ ❏

BAHAMAS

REVIEW QUESTIONS

Circle the correct answer.

1. The Bahamas became a British colony in ...

    a. 1492   b. 1600   c. 1717   d. 1838

2. Christopher Columbus landed at San Salvador in ...

    a. 1492   b. 1600   c. 1717   d. 1838

3. During the Civil War, the Bahamas were used for ...

    a. pirate hideouts   b. a British colony   c. bases for trading ships

Fill in the blanks with the correct answer.

4. From what country did the Bahamas gain its independence? _____

5. The capital city of the Bahamas is _____.

6. _____ was the first European country to claim the Bahamas.

7. Spain _____ the Lucayo Indians in order to do the work in the _____ _____ of Cuba and _____.

8. The Spanish _____ settled in the Bahamas.

9. _____ is the official language of the Bahamas today.

10. In what year did the Bahamas gain its independence? _____

11. Britain _____ slavery in the Bahamas in 1838.

12. Explain why you think tourism in the Bahamas boomed in the mid-1900's.

_____

_____

_____

_____

_____

Belize

MAP • FACTS • HISTORY and REVIEW QUESTIONS

New Words to Learn:

Find the words in a dictionary and write the meanings on the line.

1. **civilization** - _____

2. **constitution** - _____

3. **explorer** - _____

4. **flourish** - _____

5. **independence** - _____

6. **territory** - _____

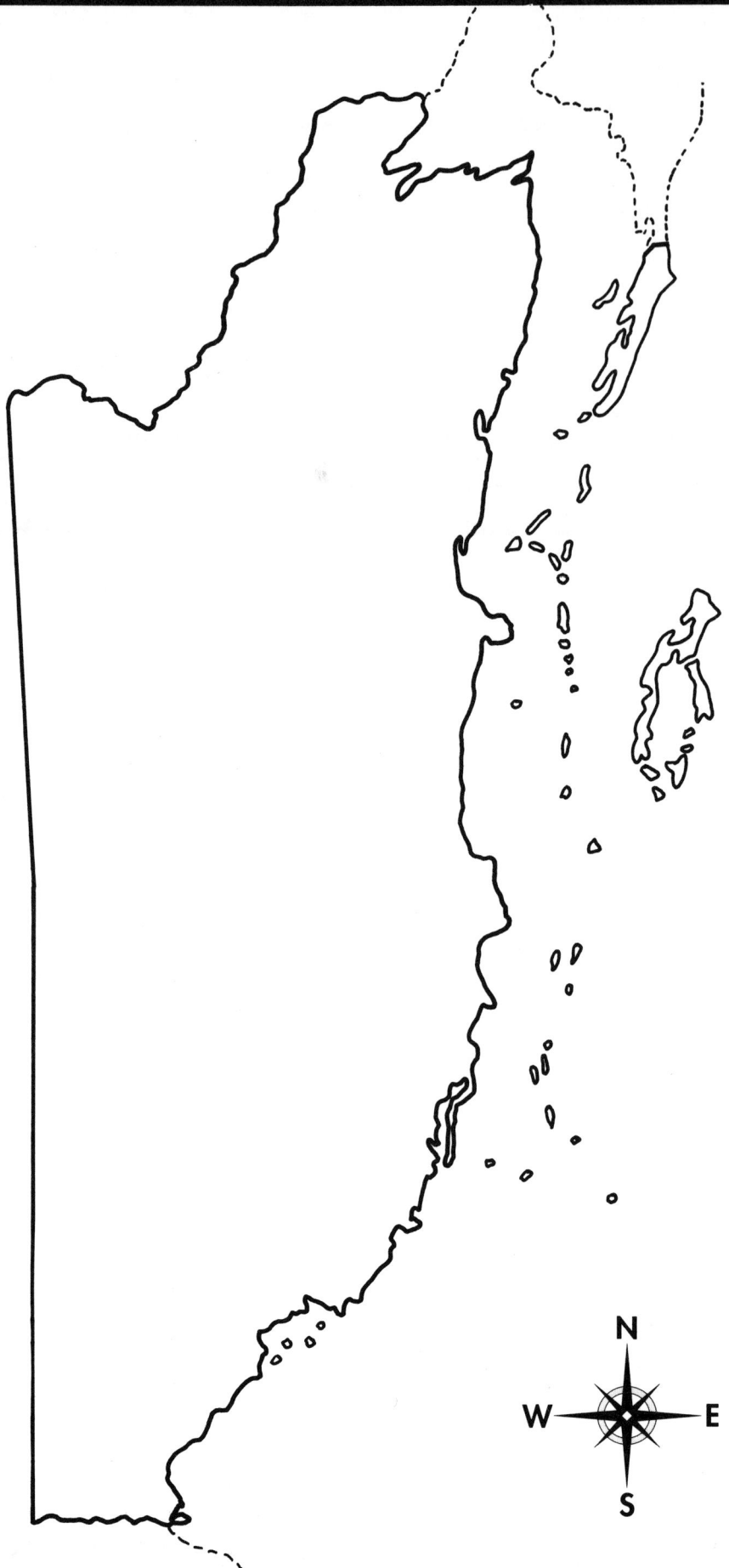

BELIZE

© GOLDEN EDUCATIONAL CENTER

BELIZE

(beh-LEEZ)

Name _____

Date _____

DATE of INDEPENDENCE: 1981, from Great Britain.

NATION'S CAPITAL CITY: Belmopan.

OFFICIAL LANGUAGE: English.

FORM of GOVERNMENT: Constitutional Monarchy.

AREA: 8,867 square miles (22,965 square kilometers).

POPULATION (est.1989): 200,000 people.   *Density*: 22 people per square mile.
9 people per square kilometer.
62% urban (city) living and 38% rural (country) living.

LARGEST CITY: Belize City - 47,000 people.

ELEVATION: *Highest*: Victoria Peak - 3,680 feet (1,122 m) above sea level.
Lowest: Sea level.

ADDITIONAL INFORMATION: Belize is part of an area that was once the great Mayan
Civilization. It is Central America's least populated country. About half of its
population has a full or partially black African ancestry. Many of the people speak
Spanish as well as English. Some of them also speak Mayan Indian languages.
• Belize has only one radio station and no television station.

Belize's Flag

Flag Description

1. The stripes on the top and bottom
   are red.

2. The broad stripe in the middle is
   dark blue.

3. Belize's coat of arms is in the
   center of the flag.

4. Color the flag the correct colors.

BELIZE
(beh-LEEz)

EARLY HISTORY in BRIEF

The Maya Indian **civilization** spread into the area of today's Belize between 1500 B.C. and A.D. 300. They came from the northern part of the Yucatán Peninsula (today, part of Mexico). The Mayan civilization **flourished** in the Belize area until around A.D. 1000. There is little known about the area from A.D. 1000 to the early 1500's. Spanish **explorers** reached the coast at this time.

In the 1520's, Spain claimed the Belize area and made it a part of the Captaincy General of Guatemala. The first known European settlement was established by British sailors who had shipwrecked. This was in 1638. During the next 150 years, Britain established several more settlements in the area. Spain did very little to establish its claim on the region. Britain gradually gained control of the area. In 1862, it named the area the Colony of British Honduras.

Great Britain made British Honduras a self-governing **territory** in 1964. In 1973, British Honduras changed its name to Belize. On September 21, 1981, Belize gained its **independence** from Great Britain. Ever since Guatemala gained its independence from Spain in 1821, it has claimed Belize as its territory. However, little has come of their claim.

❑ ❑ ❑ ❑ ❑ ❑ ❑

A young girl dressed in a garment that might look very similar to the ones her Mayan ancestors could have woven.

© GOLDEN EDUCATIONAL CENTER

BELIZE

REVIEW QUESTIONS

Circle the correct answer.

1. The official language of Belize is ...
   a. Portuguese   b. English   c. French   d. Spanish

2. Britain first called Belize ...
   a. Belize   b. Guatemala   c. New Spain   d. British Honduras

3. Belize gained its independence in ...
   a. 1500   b. 1520   c. 1973   d. 1981

Fill in the blanks with the correct answer.

4. The _____ civilization came from the _____ _____
   and settled in the area of Belize around _____ .

5. The Spanish claimed the Belize area and made it part of the _____
   _____ .

6. The first known European settlement was established by _____
   sailors who had _____ . This first European
   _____ in the area of Belize was in the year 1638.

7. Today, Belize has a _____ _____ form of government.

8. Belize's largest city, according to population, is _____ .

9. In 1821, Belize gained its independence from _____ . Ever since then,
   _____ has claimed Belize as its own _____.

10. Explain what is meant by a *monarchy*. Tell why, or why not, you would want
    to live in a country that is ruled by a monarchy form of government.

    _____

    _____

    _____

    _____

Canada

MAP • FACTS • HISTORY and REVIEW QUESTIONS

New Words to Learn:

Find the words in a dictionary and write the meanings on the line.

1. **ancestor** - _____

2. **convention** - _____

3. **escalate** - _____

4. **foothold** - _____

5. **interior** - _____

6. **province** - _____

7. **tribe** - _____

8. **royal** - _____

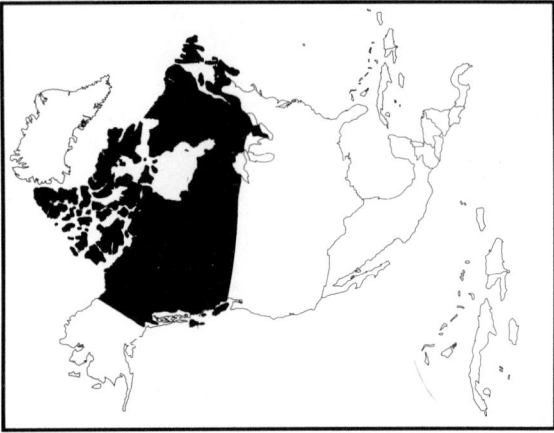

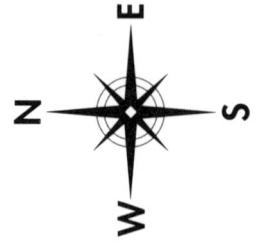

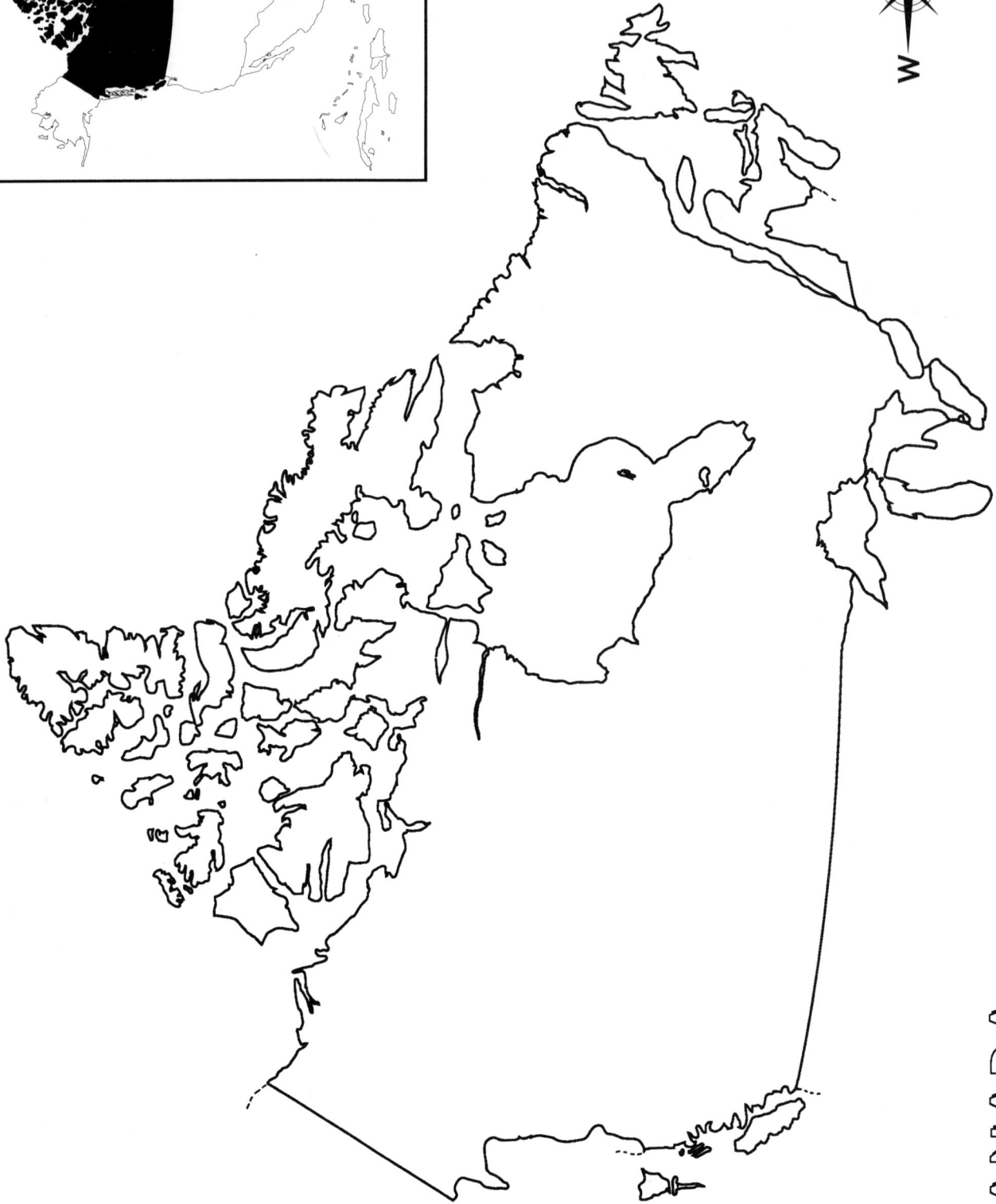

CANADA

CANADA
(CAN-uh-duh)

DATE of INDEPENDENCE: July 1, 1931, from Great Britain.

NATION'S CAPITAL CITY: Ottawa.

OFFICIAL LANGUAGE: English and French.

FORM of GOVERNMENT: Constitutional Monarchy.

AREA: The largest country in North America.
3,851,809 square miles (9,976,140 square kilometers).

POPULATION (est.1989): 26,300,000 people. *Density*: 7 people per square mile.
3 people per square kilometer.
76% urban (city) living and 24% rural (country) living.

LARGEST CITY: Toronto - 3,427,168 people.

ELEVATION: *Highest*: Mount Logan - 19,520 feet (5,950 m) above sea level.
Lowest: Sea level.

ADDITIONAL INFORMATION: The country of Canada stretches South from the North Pole to the U.S. border. Because of Canada's cold northern climate, 85% of the population lives in the southernmost regions, within 200 miles of the U.S./Canadian border. • Canada is the second largest country in the world. Only the U.S.S.R has more area. • Canada's wealth of natural resources is considered its greatest possession.

Canada's Flag

Flag Description

1. The two end sections are red and the middle section is white.

2. The maple leaf in the middle is red. It is one of Canada's national symbols.

3. Color the flag the correct colors.

CANADA
(CAN-uh-duh)

Name _____

Date _____

EARLY HISTORY in BRIEF

Indian **tribes** lived throughout Canada long before any white people arrived. Most of the tribes hunted and fished in areas that later became large Canadian cities. They called a portion of the Saint Lawrence River valley *Canada*, from an Indian word that meant a *'group of huts.'*

Vikings from Iceland were the first known white men to visit the eastern shores of Canada in the A.D. 1000's. There is evidence that they established a settlement in northern Newfoundland at L'Anse aux Meadows. The English explorer, John Cabot, sailed from England in 1497. Historians believe he landed on Newfoundland or Cape Breton Island.

In 1524, an Italian, Giovanni da Verrazano, explored the Canadian coast for France. Ten years later the French explorer, Jacques Cartier became the first European to reach the Gulf of Saint Lawrence. He claimed the surrounding area for France. A year later he sailed up the Saint Lawrence River as far inland as where Montreal is today. France paid little attention to Canada during the rest of the 1500's.

The French explorer, Samuel de Champlain, is often called the *'Father of New France.'* (The French called their North American colonies *'New France.'*) In 1608, he founded Quebec, establishing the first permanent settlement in Canada. He explored the **interior** as far as the Georgian Bay on Lake Huron. Montreal was first named Ville Marie and was founded as a missionary center in 1642.

King Louis XIV made Canada a **province** of France in 1663. Within one hundred years there were about 60,000 French settlers in Canada. They became the **ancestors** of today's French Canadians.

As a **royal** colony under French rule, the settlers had many hardships. They had to defend themselves against the Dutch, English and Iroquois Indians. Compte de Frontenac was appointed governor of the colony by the King of France. He became a leader in the fight against the Indians until the early 1700's.

CANADA
(CAN-uh-duh)

From the first years of settlement, the colonists from France and New England began fighting over the rich fur trade in the Canadian territory. However, the fighting **escalated** in 1689. The Hudson Bay Company gained a **foothold** for England on Hudson Bay in 1670. The French colony of Louisiana was established in 1699. The French then built a chain of forts to link Louisiana to New France. Great Britain gained control of Nova Scotia, Newfoundland and the Hudson Bay region as part of the *Treaty of Utrecht* in 1713. For the next 30 years there was peace in New France. This was the longest period of peace in the history of New France.

The final struggle between France and Great Britain began in 1758. The United States refers to this struggle as the *French and Indian War*. Europeans refer to this as the *Seven Years' War*. The French were winning until 1758, when the British soldiers gained control of key French positions in the interior and also captured Louisbourg. In 1759, British forces defeated the French at the Battle of Quebec. A year later, the French surrendered the colony of Montreal. Great Britain gained control of Canada in the *Treaty of Paris* in 1763. France received control of Saint Pierre and the Miquelon Islands.

The British made very few changes in the life and government of the colony. However, Canada was renamed the *Province of Quebec*. The *Revolutionary War* in the 13 American colonies left the British leaders fearful they would lose their colonies in Canada unless they ruled firmly. In the *War of 1812,* the Canadians defeated the invasions of the United States. After the war, the Canadian colonists sought self-government.

The British government sent Lord Durham to Canada to study the troubles and discontent in Canada. From Lord Durham's suggestion, in 1848, the British granted Canada limited self-government.

The *Quebec Conference of 1864* turned out to be a constitutional **convention**. The representatives who attended were called the "Fathers of Confederation." Some wanted to call the new government the *Kingdom of Canada*. However, the name *Dominion of Canada* was finally chosen. *The British North America Act* was passed by the British Parliament in 1867, joining the provinces of Canada, New Brunswick, and Nova Scotia; and forming Ontario and Quebec. It was not until July 1, 1931 that Canada became a totally independent country.

❑ ❑

CANADA

Name _____

REVIEW QUESTIONS   Date _____

Fill in the blanks with the correct answer.

1. Canada's largest city according to population is _____ .

2. In 1867, the British North America Act joined _____, _____,
   and _____ and formed _____ and Quebec.

3. _____ and _____ are the official languages of Canada.

4. Vikings from _____ were the _____ known white men to visit
   the eastern shores of Canada (North America) around the year _____.

5. What was the year Canada become an independent country? _____

6. Explain how Canada got its name and what it means.

   _____

   _____

   _____

7. Why were the British leaders so insistent on ruling Canada firmly?

   _____

   _____

   _____

   _____

8. Explain the struggle (and outcome) over Canada between France and England.

   _____

   _____

   _____

   _____

   _____

9. List the names of Canada from the time the French first explored the territory.

   _____

   _____

Costa Rica

MAP • FACTS • HISTORY and REVIEW QUESTIONS

New Words to Learn:

Find the words in a dictionary and write the meanings on the line.

1. **archeology** - _____

2. **empire** - _____

3. **game** - _____

4. **literate** - _____

5. **migrate** - _____

6. **republic** - _____

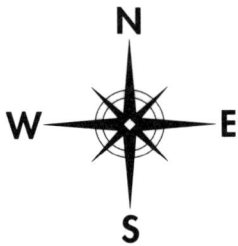

COSTA RICA

© Golden Educational Center

COSTA RICA

(KOS-tuh REE-kuh)

Name _____

Date _____

DATE of INDEPENDENCE: September 15, 1821, from Spain; 1823, from Mexico. 1838, actually declared independence.

NATION'S CAPITAL CITY: San José.

OFFICIAL LANGUAGE: Spanish.

FORM of GOVERNMENT: Republic.

AREA: 19,652 square miles   (50,898 square kilometers).

POPULATION (est. 1989): 3,000,000 people. _Density:_ 153 people per square mile. 59 people per square kilometer. 41% urban (city) living and 59% rural (country) living.

LARGEST CITY: San José - 278,500 people.

ELEVATION: _Highest:_ Chirripó Grande - 12,530 feet (3,819 m) above sea level. _Lowest:_ Sea level on the coastline.

ADDITIONAL INFORMATION: The Guaymi Indians inhabited Costa Rica when the Spaniards arrived in the 1500's. • Almost all of today's Costa Ricans are of a mixed Spanish and Indian blood line. • Costa Rica has a fairly high standard of living. • It is a mostly agricultural country with coffee as its chief export. • About 93% of the country's people are **literate**, the highest percent in all of Central America.

Costa Rica's Flag

Flag Description

1. The top and bottom stripes of Costa Rica's flag are bright blue. The center stripe is red and the other two stripes are white.

2. Costa Rica's coat of arms is in the middle stripe on the flag.

3. Color the flag the correct colors.

COSTA RICA

(KOS-tuh REE-kuh)

Name _____

Date _____

EARLY HISTORY in BRIEF

Indians were the first people to live in the area that is today Costa Rica. **Archeologists** know that by the year A.D. 1000, the Corobicí tribe had settled in the northern valleys. The Boruca had **migrated** to the southern area of the region. The Carib, Chorotega, and Nahau Indians came to the area in the 1400's. Most of these Indians raised crops and hunted small **game** to live.

Christopher Columbus arrived in Costa Rica in 1502. Many Spaniards moved to the region because of a rumor of gold in the area. The rumor was false. However, many of them stayed to become farmers in the Central Highlands. The first permanent, white settlement was at Cartago in 1564. Many Spaniards tried to enslave the Indians. However, most of the tribes fought hard to stay free.

Costa Rica remained a Spanish colony for several hundred years. In 1821, Spain's other Central American colonies, along with Costa Rica, broke away from Spanish rule. The next year they joined the Mexican **empire**. A year later these same Central American states withdrew from Mexico and formed the United Provinces of Central America. In 1838, this Union began to collapse and Costa Rica declared its independence.

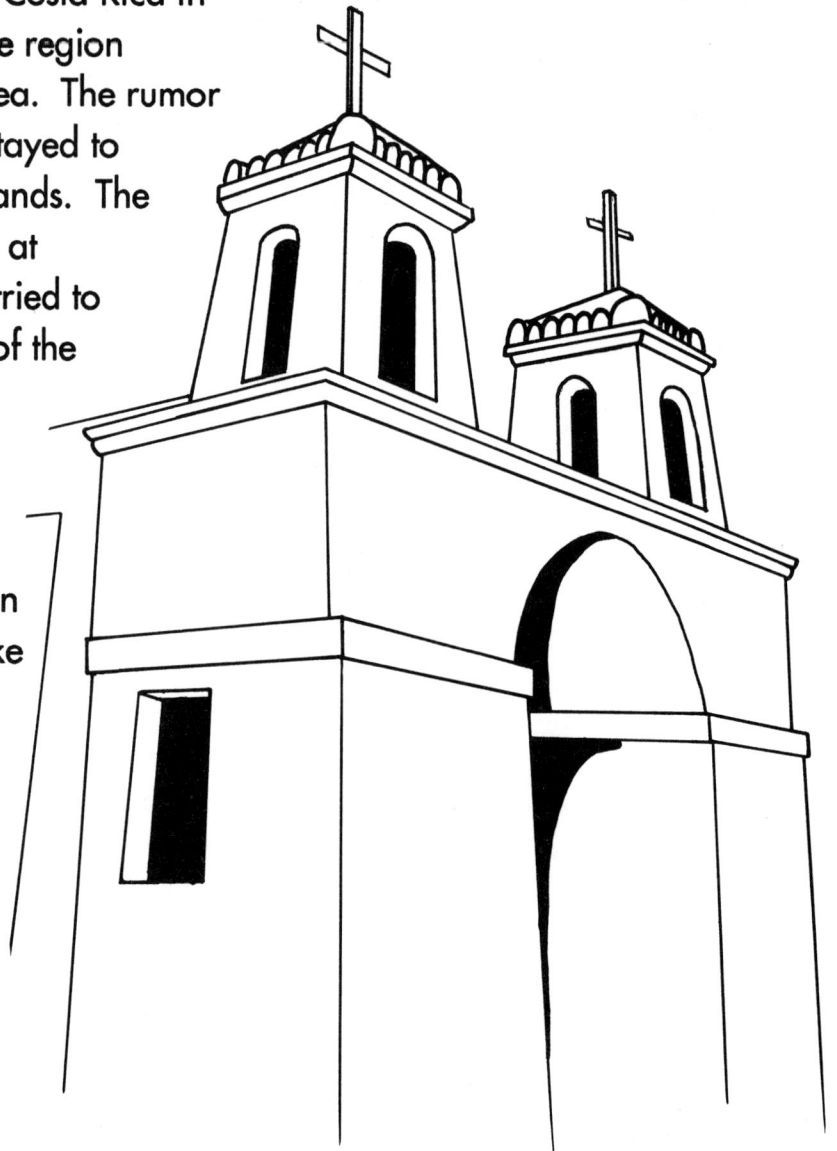

❑ ❑ ❑ ❑ ❑ ❑ ❑

A Catholic church that was established in Costa Rica by early Spanish settlers and priests.

© GOLDEN EDUCATIONAL CENTER

COSTA RICA

Name _____

Date _____

Circle the correct answer.

1. The Indians living in the Costa Rica area were there by the year ...
   a. 1500   b. 1400   c. 1000   d. 500

2. The official language of Costa Rica is ...
   a. French   b. Spanish   c. Rican   d. English

3. Today's government of Costa Rica is ...
   a. Democracy   b. Monarchy   c. Republic   d. Dictatorship

Fill in the blanks with the correct answer.

4. The capital city of Costa Rica is _____ . According to
   _____ it is also Costa Rica's _____ city.

5. _____ arrived in Costa Rica in 1502.

6. The first _____ white settlement was at _____ in 1526.

7. In 1822, Costa Rica joined the _____ empire.

8. Many of the Spaniards tried to _____ the _____.
   However, they _____ hard to stay free.

9. What year did Costa Rica gain its independence? _____

10. From what country did Costa Rica gain its independence? _____

11. Explain why many Spaniards moved to the area of Costa Rica in the early 1500's.

   _____

   _____

   _____

   _____

   _____

Cuba

MAP • FACTS • HISTORY and REVIEW QUESTIONS

New Words to Learn:

Find the words in a dictionary and write the meanings on the line.

1. **brutal** - _____

2. **dictator** - _____

3. **dwindle** - _____

4. **import** - _____

5. **native** - _____

6. **political** - _____

7. **reform** - _____

8. **revolt** - _____

9. **stockpiling** - _____

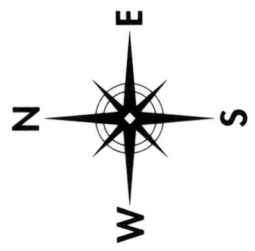

N E S W

CUBA

CUBA
(KYOO-buh)

DATE of INDEPENDENCE: 1902, from the United States. (Spain had initial control of Cuba.)

NATION'S CAPITAL CITY: Havana.

OFFICIAL LANGUAGE: Spanish.

FORM of GOVERNMENT: Socialist/Republic (Official).
                                            Dictatorship (Actual).

AREA: 44,218 square miles   (114,524 square kilometers).

POPULATION (est.1989): 10,500,000 people.   _Density_: 237 people per square mile.
                                                    92 people per square kilometer.
                        60% urban (city) living and 40% rural (country) living.

LARGEST CITY: Havana - 2,013,746 people.

ELEVATION: _Highest_: Pico Turquino - 6,542 feet (5,775 m) above sea level.
                    Lowest: Sea level.

ADDITIONAL INFORMATION: Cuba consists of one large island and about 1600 smaller
        ones. Cubans call their island the _Pearl of the Antilles_ because it is so beautiful. • In
        1959, Fidel Castro overthrew the existing government and later set up a Communist
        government with himself as the head of it. • In 1962, the United States almost went
        to war against Cuba (and the U.S.S.R) because of the missiles Cuba was **stockpiling**.

Cuba's Flag

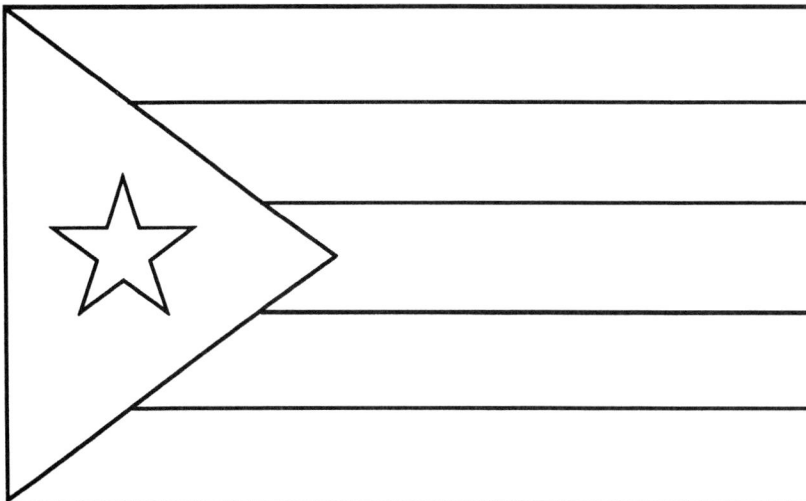

Flag Description

1. The stripes on Cuba's flag alternate, in color, from the top to bottom with the top one being dark blue and the next one being white.

2. The triangle on the left is red with a white star in the middle of it.

3. Color the flag the correct colors.

CUBA
(KYOO-buh)

EARLY HISTORY in BRIEF

Christopher Columbus landed in Cuba in 1492 and claimed it for Spain. Spanish people began to settle the island in 1511. Cuba soon became one of the richest colonies in the West Indies.

Most of the settlers became farmers and established large plantations. Their main crops were sugar and tobacco. The plantation owners forced the **native** American Indians to work in the fields. Thousands of these enslaved Indians died from harsh treatment and diseases. As the Indian population **dwindled**, the Spaniards began to **import** African slaves. The first African slaves arrived in Cuba in 1517.

Cuba developed slowly from the mid-1500's to the late 1700's. Pirates often raided the coastal settlements. These raids caused many of the colonists to move to South America. In the late 1700's Cuba became a shipyard and naval base. It began to sell its sugar and tobacco to the British colonies in North America.

Cuban plantation owners imported more and more slaves in the 1800's. Many owners treated their slaves **brutally**. In 1812, a group of slaves **revolted** against their owners. However, their efforts did not help, and the Spaniards hanged the revolting slaves.

In 1821, José Francisco Lemus organized the first major revolt against Spanish rule in Cuba. However, the movement collapsed in five years. In the mid-1800's the United States offered to buy Cuba from Spain several different times, but Spain would not sell.

Cuba's struggle against Spanish rule led to the beginning of the *Ten Years' War* in 1868. At the end of the war a treaty was signed *(Pact of Zanjón)* that provided for the gradual ending of slavery and **political reform**. Slavery was totally abolished in 1886.

As a result of the Spanish-American War, Cuba was under U.S. military control from 1898 to 1902. Cuban people elected the first president of the newly formed Republic of Cuba in 1902.

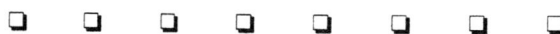

❑ ❑ ❑ ❑ ❑ ❑ ❑ ❑

CUBA

REVIEW QUESTIONS

Circle the correct answer.

1. Cuba was a colony of ...
   a. Spain   b. United States   c. France   d. Great Britain

2. The official language of Cuba is ...
   a. English   b. Mayan   c. French   d. Spanish

3. Cuba quickly became one of the richest colonies in ...
   a. New Spain   b. Atlantic Ocean   c. West Indies   d. Spain

Fill in the blanks with the correct answer.

4. In what year did Cuba gain its independence? _____

5. The main crops of the plantations were _____ and _____.
   The owners _____ the Indians and thousands _____
   from _____ and _____ treatment.

6. _____ first landed on Cuba in 1492.

7. From what country did Cuba gain its independence? _____

8. What did the Spaniards do to the slaves who revolted against their owners?
   _____

9. What was one of the results from the Spanish-American War?
   _____
   _____

10. Explain what the *Pact of Zanjón* was and what it finally accomplished.
   _____
   _____
   _____
   _____

Dominican Republic

MAP • FACTS • HISTORY and REVIEW QUESTIONS

New Words to Learn:

Find the words in a dictionary and write the meanings on the line.

1. **export** - _____

2. **flagship** - _____

3. **income** - _____

4. **influence** - _____

5. **scarcity** - _____

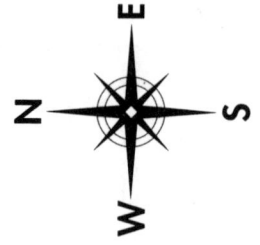

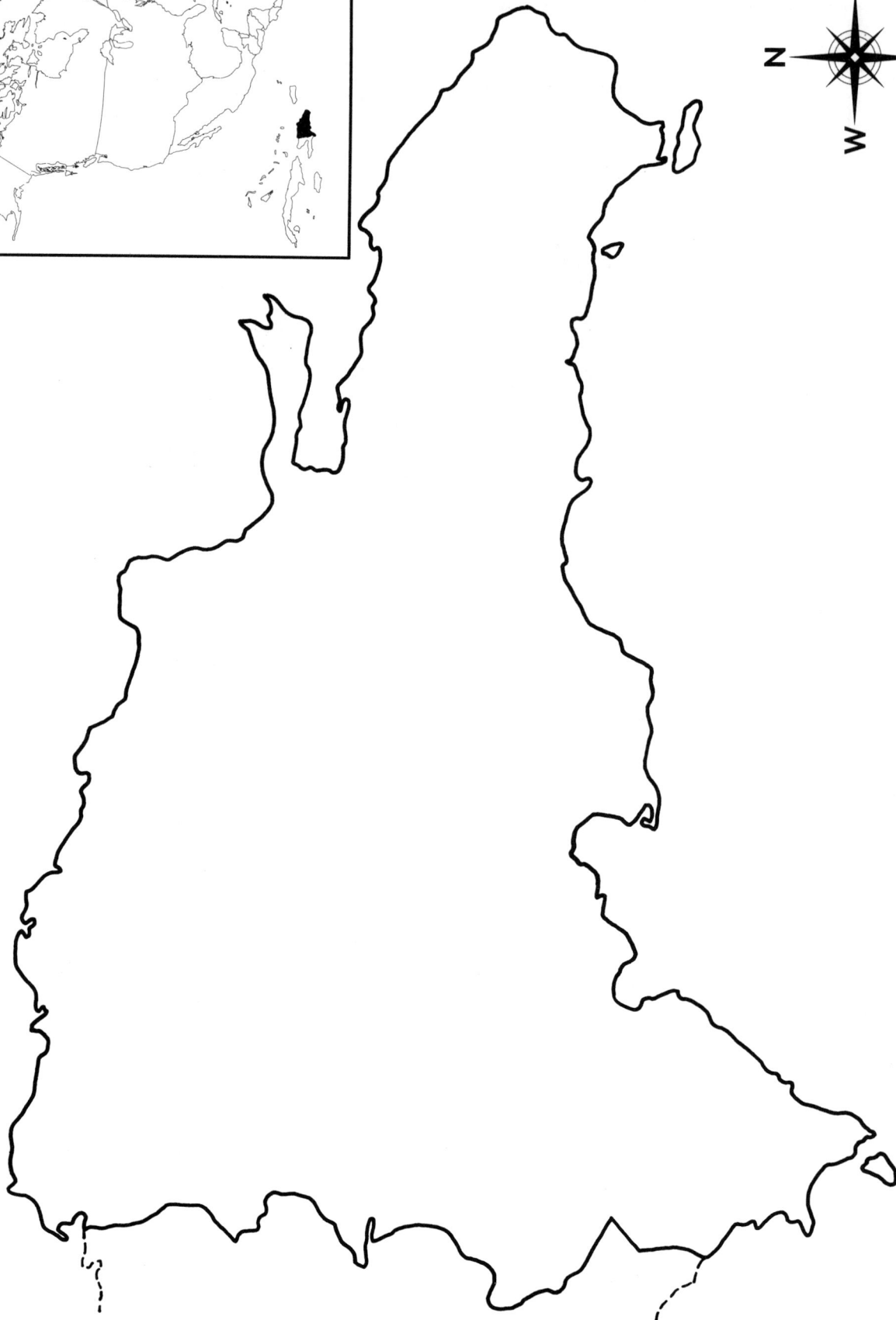

DOMINICAN REPBUBLIC

DOMINICAN REPUBLIC

(DOH-min-i-kan REE-puhb-lic)

Name _____

Date _____

DATE of INDEPENDENCE: 1822, from Spain.
(From 1861 to 1865, Spain governed the country.)

NATION'S CAPITAL CITY: Santo Domingo.

OFFICIAL LANGUAGE: Spanish.

FORM of GOVERNMENT: Republic.

AREA: 18,704 square miles   (48,443 square kilometers).

POPULATION (est 1989): 7,000,000 people.   _Density:_ 374 people per square mile.
144 people per square kilometer.
49% urban (city) living and 51% rural (country) living.

LARGEST CITY: Santo Domingo - 1,410,000 people.

ELEVATION: _Highest:_ Duarte Peak - 10,417 feet (3,175 m) above sea level.
Lowest: Lake Enriquillo - 150 feet 46 m) below sea level.

ADDITIONAL INFORMATION: The country's name in Spanish, the official language, is _República Dominicana._ • The United States occupied the country two times in the 1900's to stop fighting between political parties trying to gain control of the country's government. • Sugar is the country's leading source of **income,** with about three-fourths of it being **exported** to the United States.

Dominican Republic's Flag

Flag Description

1. The cross stripe on the flag is white and stands for salvation.

2. The four rectangles alternate dark blue and red with blue being in the upper left hand corner. Blue represents liberty and red the blood of heroes.

3. The coat of arms is in the center of the flag.

4. Color the flag the correct colors.

DOMINICAN REPUBLIC

(DOH-min-i-kan REE-puhb-lic)

EARLY HISTORY in BRIEF

Christopher Columbus explored several islands in the Caribbean Sea during his first voyage to the region. He landed on the island of Hispaniola on December 6, 1492 on his first voyage to the New World. He claimed the area for Spain. Haiti covers the island's western end. The Dominican Republic is in the eastern portion of the island.

Columbus had his men build Fort Navidad on the northern end of the island. They used the ruins of his **flagship**, the *Santa Maria*. He returned a year later with 1,300 men to find the island's gold. Columbus found the Indians of the island had killed his men and destroyed the fort. Several years later, thousands of Spanish colonists came to the island and soon conquered the native Indians. Many of these settlers also established towns on the northern coast.

The country's capital is Santo Domingo. It was the first city in the Western Hemisphere founded by Europeans. It was founded by the Spanish in 1496, and originally named La Nueva Isabela. Some historians believe that Columbus was buried in the Cathedral of Santo Domingo. The University of Santo Domingo was established in 1538. It is the oldest university in the Western Hemisphere.

By the mid-1500's, the **scarcity** of gold in Hispaniola **influenced** the Spanish settlers to move to Cuba, Mexico and Peru. The island's population was reduced to about 30,000 people. In 1606, Spain ordered all of its settlers to move into the area. Ninety-one years later, in 1697, Spain turned over the western third of the island (now Haiti) to France.

Black slaves from Haiti rebelled against their French masters and conquered the entire island in 1801. France and Spain briefly recovered their colonies later that same year. The Haitians regained control of the island in 1822. In 1844, the Dominicans successfully broke away from Haitian rule. At the Dominicans' request, Spain governed the country from 1861 to 1865, in order to protect it from the Haitians.

❏ ❏

DOMINICAN REPUBLIC

Name _____

Circle the correct answer.

1. The official language of the Dominican Republic is ...
    a. Portuguese   b. Spanish   c. French   d. English

2. The Dominican Republic is located on which side of the island of Hispaniola?
    a. North   b. East   c. West   d. South

3. The Dominican Republic gained its independence from ...
    a. England   b. France   c. Spain   d. Portugal

Fill in the blanks with the correct answer.

4. Christopher Columbus landed on the island on his _____ _____.

5. The _____ university in the Western _____ is the
    _____, located in Santo Domingo.

6. The _____ city in the _____ Hemisphere is Santo Domingo.

7. The capital city of the Dominican Republic is _____ .

8. The Dominican Republic is located in which body of water? _____

9. The Dominican Republic is part of what island? _____

10. Describe the flag of the Dominican Republic and tell what the symbols and colors mean.

    _____

    _____

    _____

    _____

    _____

El Salvador

MAP • FACTS • HISTORY and REVIEW QUESTIONS

New Words to Learn:

Find the words in a dictionary and write the meanings on the line.

1. **descendants** - _____

2. **democracy** - _____

3. **federation** - _____

4. **fierce** - _____

5. **limestone** - _____

6. **mineral** - _____

7. **pyramid** - _____

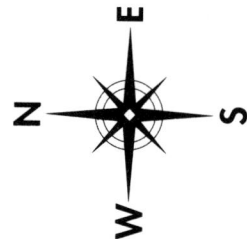

EL SALVADOR

EL SALVADOR

(ehl-SAL-vuh dawr)

Name _____

Date _____

DATE of INDEPENDENCE: September 15, 1821, from Spain; 1823, from Mexico.
1841, actually declared independence.

NATION'S CAPITAL CITY: San Salvador.

OFFICIAL LANGUAGE: Spanish.

FORM of GOVERNMENT: Democratic Republic (**Democracy**).

AREA: 8,260 square miles (21,393 square kilometers).

POPULATION (est. 1989): 5,100,000 people.   _Density_: 617 people per square mile.
238 people per square kilometer.
39% urban (city) living and 61% rural (country) living.

LARGEST CITY: San Salvador - 459,902 people.

ELEVATION: _Highest_: Monte Cristo - 7,933 feet (2,418 m) above sea level.
Lowest: Sea level along the coast.

ADDITIONAL INFORMATION: El Salvador is the smallest Central American country in area. However, only Guatemala has more people. • Because of the rapid growth in population the good farmland is almost all used. More than half of the nation's people are farmers. Coffee is the country's most important crop. • Many of the Indians of El Salvador are **descendants** of the Pipil Indians.

El Salvador's Flag

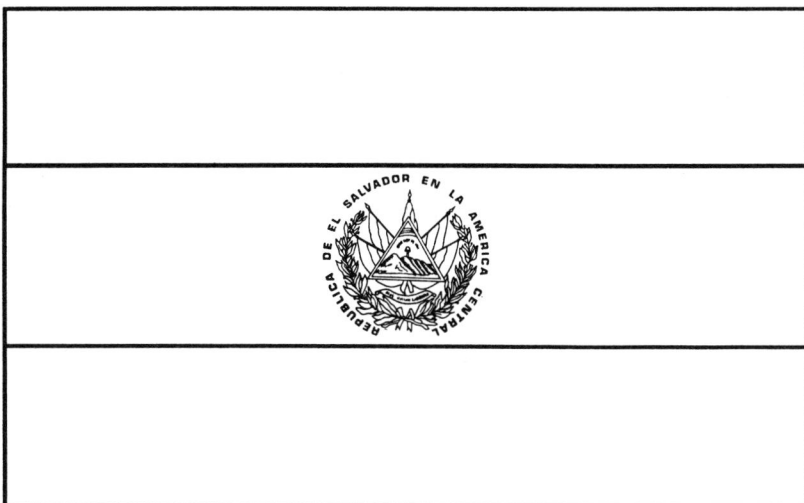

Flag Description

1. The top and bottom stripes are blue and the middle stripe is white.

2. Blue symbolizes unity and the white stripe represents peace.

3. The coat of arms is in the center of the flag.

4. Color the flag the correct colors.

EL SALVADOR
(ehl-SAL-vuh-dawr)

Name _____

Date _____

EARLY HISTORY in BRIEF

Indians were the first people to live in the area known today as El Salvador. Nahua Indians came from Mexico as early as 3000 B.C. Other Indian tribes later settled in the area. In western El Salvador, the ruins of huge **limestone pyramids** built by the Maya Indians between A.D. 100 and A.D. 1000 still stand. The Pipil tribe took control of the western part of the region during the 1000's. They built cities, raised crops and were very good weavers of baskets, blankets and other objects.

In 1524, Spanish soldiers invaded El Salvador. A year later, after long and **fierce** fighting, the Spanish defeated the Pipil and other Indian tribes. El Salvador remained a Spanish colony for almost 300 years. There was very little **mineral** wealth in the region. Therefore, El Salvador attracted fewer settlers than Spain's other colonies in the New World. Most of the settlers in the region farmed the land and raised cattle.

In 1821, El Salvador and Spain's other colonial holdings in Central America broke away from Spanish rule. This group of colonies wrote a constitution and formed a **federation** in 1823. They called the federation the United Provinces of Central America. The federation began to collapse in 1838. El Salvador declared its independence in 1841.

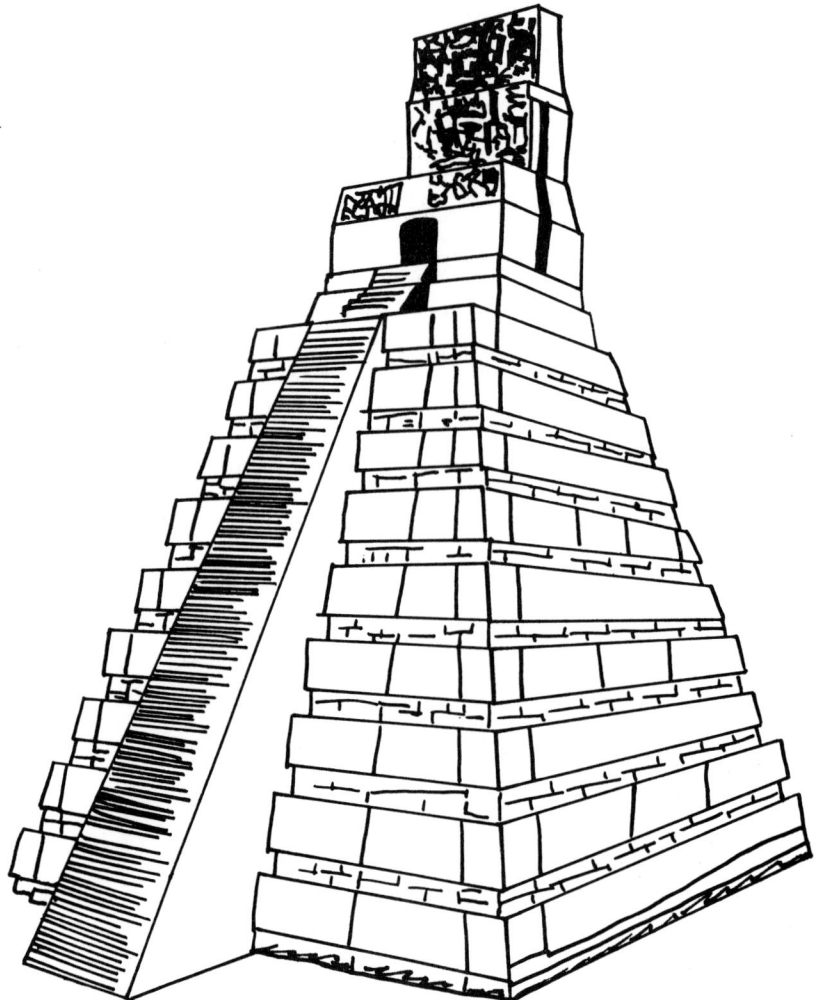

❑   ❑   ❑   ❑   ❑   ❑   ❑

This is an artist's idea of how an ancient Mayan pyramid might have looked.

© GOLDEN EDUCATIONAL CENTER

EL SALVADOR

REVIEW QUESTIONS

Circle the correct answer.

1. El Salvador was a Spanish colony for approximately how many years?
   a. 3000   b. 1000   c. 300   d. 100

2. Spanish soldiers invaded the Pipil and other Indian tribes in ...
   a. 1524   b. 1821   c. 1823   d. 1838

3. How many years after the Nahua Indians came to the area did the Spanish arrive?
   a. 1000   b. 3000   c. 1524   d. 4524

Fill in the blanks with the correct answer.

4. In what year did El Salvador gain its independence? _____

5. From what country did El Salvador gain its independence? _____

6. The Pipil Indians took control of the _____ region during the 1000's.
   They built _____, raised _____ and were very good
   _____ .

7. What form of government does El Salvador have today? _____ .

8. The capital city of El Salvador is _____ .

9. Pretend you are a Native Indian whose ancestors have lived in the area of El Salvador
   for hundreds of years. Explain how you would have felt and what you would have
   done when the Spanish came into your area and took your land, killed your friends
   and made you a slave.

   _____

   _____

   _____

   _____

   _____

   _____

Guatemala

MAP • FACTS • HISTORY and REVIEW QUESTIONS

New Words to Learn:

Find the words in a dictionary and write the meanings on the line.

1. **administrator** - _____

2. **cultivate** - _____

3. **dictator** - _____

4. **expedition** - _____

5. **society** - _____

GUATEMALA

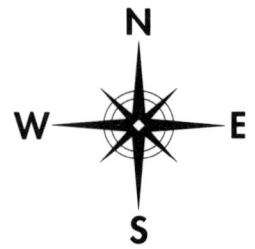

N
W · E
S

© GOLDEN EDUCATIONAL CENTER

GUATEMALA

(gwah-teh-MAH-lah)

Name _____

Date _____

DATE of INDEPENDENCE: September 15, 1821, from Spain; 1823, from Mexico.
1839, actually declared independence.

NATION'S CAPITAL CITY: Guatemala City.

OFFICIAL LANGUAGE: Spanish.

FORM of GOVERNMENT: Republic (**Dictatorship** - Actual).

AREA: 42,042 square miles (108,888 square kilometers).

POPULATION (est. 1988): 8,900,000 people.   *Density:* 212 people per square mile.
82 people per square kilometer.
36% urban (city) living and 64% rural (country) living.

LARGEST CITY: Guatemala City - 1,250,000 people.

ELEVATION: *Highest:* Volcán Tajumulco - 13,845 feet (830 m) above sea level.
Lowest: Sea level along the coasts.

ADDITIONAL INFORMATION: Guatemala is the most populated country in Central
America. Almost half of the people are Indians, of which many are ancestors of the
Maya Indians. Many of them still speak Indian languages and wear Indian clothing.
• About 5% of the coffee used in the U.S. comes from Guatemala. • Only about 30%
of the country's population can read and write.

Guatemala's Flag

Flag Description

1. The left and right portions of
Guatemala's flag are blue. The
middle section is white.

2. The blue stripes represent the
Pacific and Atlantic Oceans which
form the borders of the country.

3. The coat of arms is in the center
of the flag.

4. Color the flag the correct colors.

GUATEMALA
(gwah-teh-MAH-lah)

Name _____

Date _____

EARLY HISTORY in BRIEF

Historians know very little about the people who lived in the region that is now Guatemala before 1000 B.C. The earliest well-known **society** was located at Las Charcas in the Highlands region. The people **cultivated** corn, made pottery, and wove mats, ropes and other materials.

Part of the great Maya Indian civilization thrived in the area of Guatemala between A.D. 250 and 900. The Mayans recorded important dates on tall, carved blocks of stone called *stelae* and used a kind of picture writing. They built several centers believed to be used for their religion. These centers included beautiful palaces and pyramids. These structures were all built with limestone. Historians do not know why the Mayans abandoned these centers. When the Spaniards arrived, most of the Mayans were living in the Highlands region.

In 1523, a Spanish **expedition** set out from New Spain (the Spanish colony of Mexico) and invaded Guatemala. The Spanish soldiers defeated the major Indian groups in the area. They soon established Spanish settlement and rule in Guatemala.

About 50 years after Spain took control of Guatemala, the Spanish government set up the *Audiencia of Guatemala*. This was a high court of judges and **administrators** located in what is now the city of Antigua. This court ruled most of Central America. At this time, Guatemala was still a part of the Spanish colony of New Spain. The *Audiencia of Guatemala* had a lot of power because it was so far from the colonial capital of Mexico City. In 1776, the *Audiencia of Guatemala* moved to Guatemala City after an earthquake had destroyed most of Antigua.

On September 15, 1821, Guatemala, along with other colonies of Central America, declared their independence from Spain. They later became part of the Mexican Empire. In 1823, they broke away and formed the United Provinces of Central America. Guatemala left the Union in 1839 and became an independent country.

❑ ❑

GUATEMALA

Name _____

REVIEW QUESTIONS

Date _____

Fill in the blanks with the correct answer.

1. Guatemala has a _____ form of government.

2. The _____ were the first European settlers in Guatemala.

3. When did Guatemala become an independent country? _____

4. The capital city of Guatemala is _____ . According to _____ , it is the largest city of the country.

5. Describe what Guatemala's flag looks like and what the colors symbolize.

   _____

   _____

   _____

6. Pretend you are a Mayan Indian living in the area of Guatemala. Tell what it was like to live there and some of the reasons your people moved away and abandoned the religious centers

   _____

   _____

   _____

   _____

   _____

   _____

   _____

   _____

   _____

   _____

   _____

   _____

Haiti

MAP • FACTS • HISTORY
and REVIEW QUESTIONS

New Words to Learn:

Find the words in a dictionary and write the meanings on the line.

1. **crew** - _____

2. **inhumane** - _____

3. **yellow fever** - _____

4. **mulatto** - _____

5. **proclaim** - _____

6. **prosperous** - _____

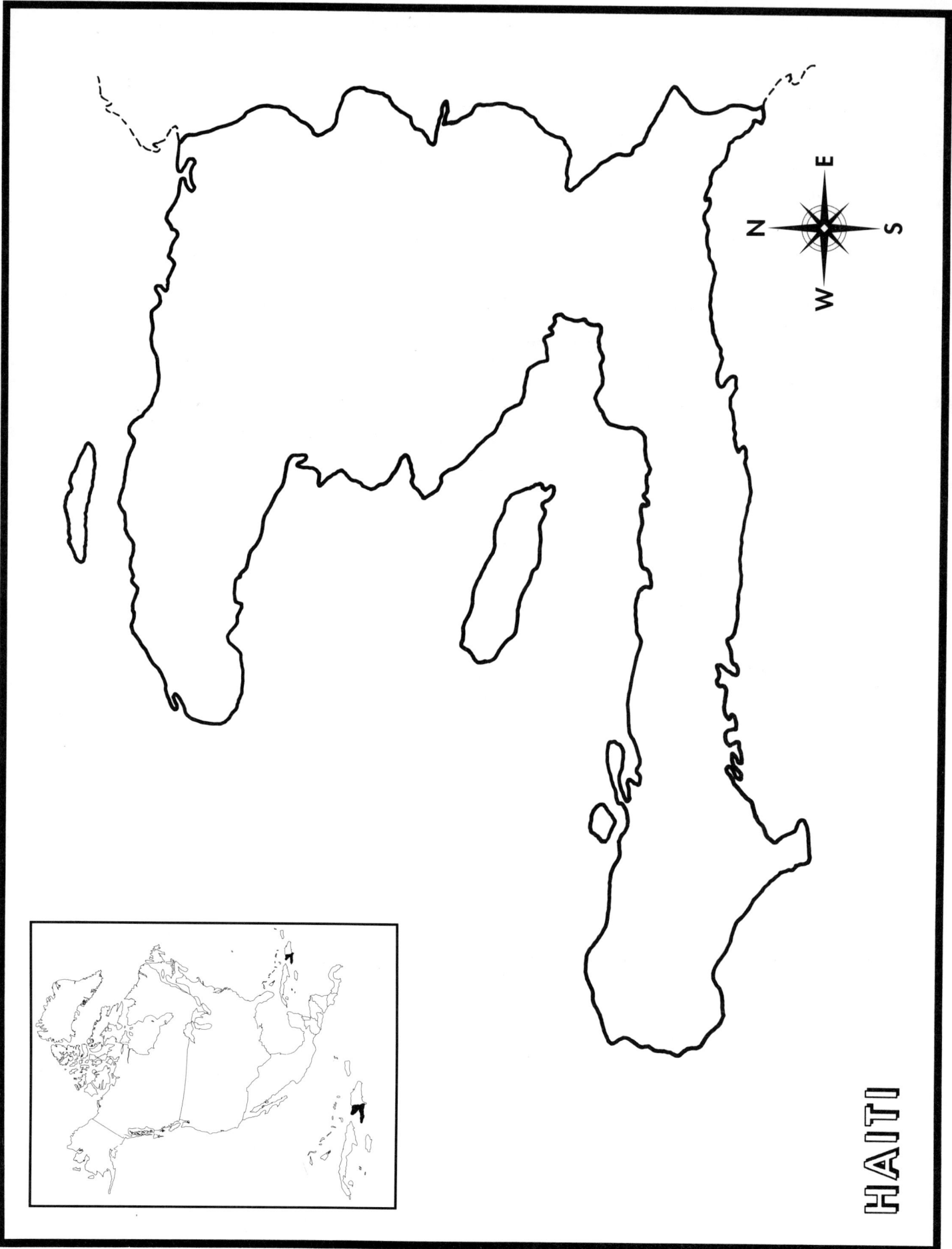

HAITI

HAITI

(HAY-tee)

Name _____

Date _____

DATE of INDEPENDENCE: January 1, 1804, from France.

NATION'S CAPITAL CITY: Port-au-Prince.

OFFICIAL LANGUAGE: French.

FORM of GOVERNMENT: Republic (Dictatorship - Actual).

AREA: 10,714 square miles (27,749 square kilometers).

POPULATION (est. 1989): 6,400,000 people.   *Density:* 597 people per square mile.
231 people per square kilometer.
24% urban (city) living and 76% rural (country) living.

LARGEST CITY: Port-au-Prince - 461,464 people.

ELEVATION: *Highest:* Pic La Selle - 8,783 feet (2,677 m) above sea level.
Lowest: Sea level.

ADDITIONAL INFORMATION: The name *Haiti* comes from an Indian word meaning *high ground.* It was named this because of the rugged mountains that cover the country. • Haiti is one of the least developed nations in the Western Hemisphere. • It is also one of the most densely populated countries in the hemisphere. • Haiti is the oldest Negro (black) republic in the world and the second oldest free nation in the Western Hemisphere. It has been independent since 1804.

Haiti's Flag

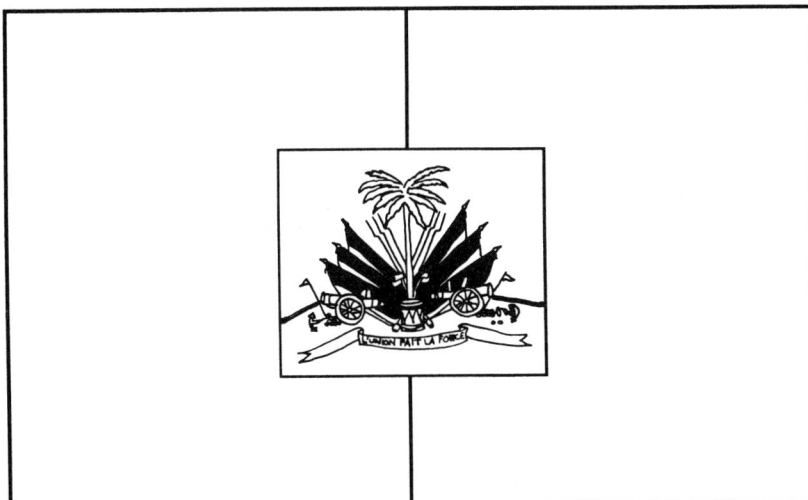

Flag Description

1. The black, left half of the flag represents the black people of Haiti. The red half represents the **mulatto** people. *(National Flag)*

2. In the center of the *State Flag* there is the country's coat of arms.

3. Color the flag the correct colors.

HAITI

(HAY-tee)

EARLY HISTORY in BRIEF

Christopher Columbus landed on the island of Hispaniola in 1492 and claimed the area for Spain. Haiti covers the island's western end. The Dominican Republic is the eastern portion of the island. One of his ships, the *Santa Maria*, ran aground on reefs near the present-day city of Cap-Haïtien on Christmas Day. His **crew** used the wood from the wreckage to build a fort. Columbus named it Fort Navidad. Some of his men stayed to man the fort while his other ships sailed on to explore other nearby islands. However, the Arawak Indians who were living on the island and these men got into a fight. Columbus' men were all killed and the fort was destroyed.

Columbus discovered gold in what is now Haiti and the Dominican Republic. Many Spanish settlers rushed to the island in hopes of finding their fortunes. These European settlers enslaved the Indians to mine their gold and grow their food. The Spanish treated the Indians so **inhumanely** that in a short 42 years there were only a few hundred Indians still alive. The settlers then began bringing slaves from Africa to do their hard work.

After several years, most of the Spanish settlers were leaving Hispaniola for more prosperous Spanish settlements in Peru and Mexico. By the early 1600's, there were so few Spanish settlers that the King of Spain ordered all of them to move closer to the city Santo Domingo, in what is now the Dominican Republic.

A worker on a sugar plantation.

HAITI
(HAY-tee)

Name _____

Date _____

Dutch, English and French pirates soon took over the area of northern Haiti. These pirates used the island of Tortuga as a base for attacking ships carrying gold and silver back to Spain. The Spanish tried, but failed, to drive the pirates out of the area.

The French took control of the western third of the island in 1697. France named this new colony Saint Domingue. French colonists brought in thousands of African slaves in order to do the work on their huge coffee and spice plantations. By 1788, there were almost one-half million slaves in Haiti. This was eight times the number of French settlers. The colony became very **prosperous** selling its plantation products to other parts of the world. This prosperity made Haiti more important to France than her Canadian colony.

During the French Revolution, in 1791, the slaves in Saint-Domingue rebelled against their French owners. The rebelling slaves destroyed several plantations and small towns. A former slave named Toussaint L'Ouverture took control of the government for a few years. Napoleon came to power in France in 1799. He quickly sent an army to Hispaniola to restore colonial rule. Toussaint was captured and imprisoned in France. However, many of the French soldiers caught **yellow fever** and died. This allowed the rebelling armies to defeat the French soldiers in 1803. On January 1, 1804, the colony **proclaimed** itself an independent country named Haiti.

❏ ❏ ❏ ❏ ❏ ❏ ❏ ❏

Former slave: Francois-Dominique Toussaint L'Ouverture

HAITI

REVIEW QUESTIONS   Date _____

Circle the correct answer.

1. After 1697, Haiti was ruled by ...

   a. France   b. Great Britain   c. Spain   d. itself

2. There were almost 500,000 black slaves in Haiti by ...

   a. 1697   b. 1788   c. 1791   d. 1799

3. The first known white person to visit the area was the ...

   a. Arawak   b. Toussaint L'Ouverture   c. Napolean   d. Columbus

Fill in the blanks with the correct answer.

4. Today, Haiti is actually a _____ form of government.

5. Haiti is on the _____ side of the island of Hispaniola .

6. Haiti gained its independence from _____ on _____ .

7. In your own words, tell what happened to the *Santa Maria* and its men.

   _____

   _____

   _____

   _____

   _____

8. Explain what happened to the Arawak Indians and why.

   _____

   _____

9. Explain why Haiti was more important to France than its Canadian colony.

   _____

   _____

   _____

Honduras

MAP • FACTS • HISTORY
and REVIEW QUESTIONS

New Words to Learn:

Find the words in a dictionary and write the meanings on the line.

1. **depth** - _____

2. **illiterate** - _____

3. **temple** - _____

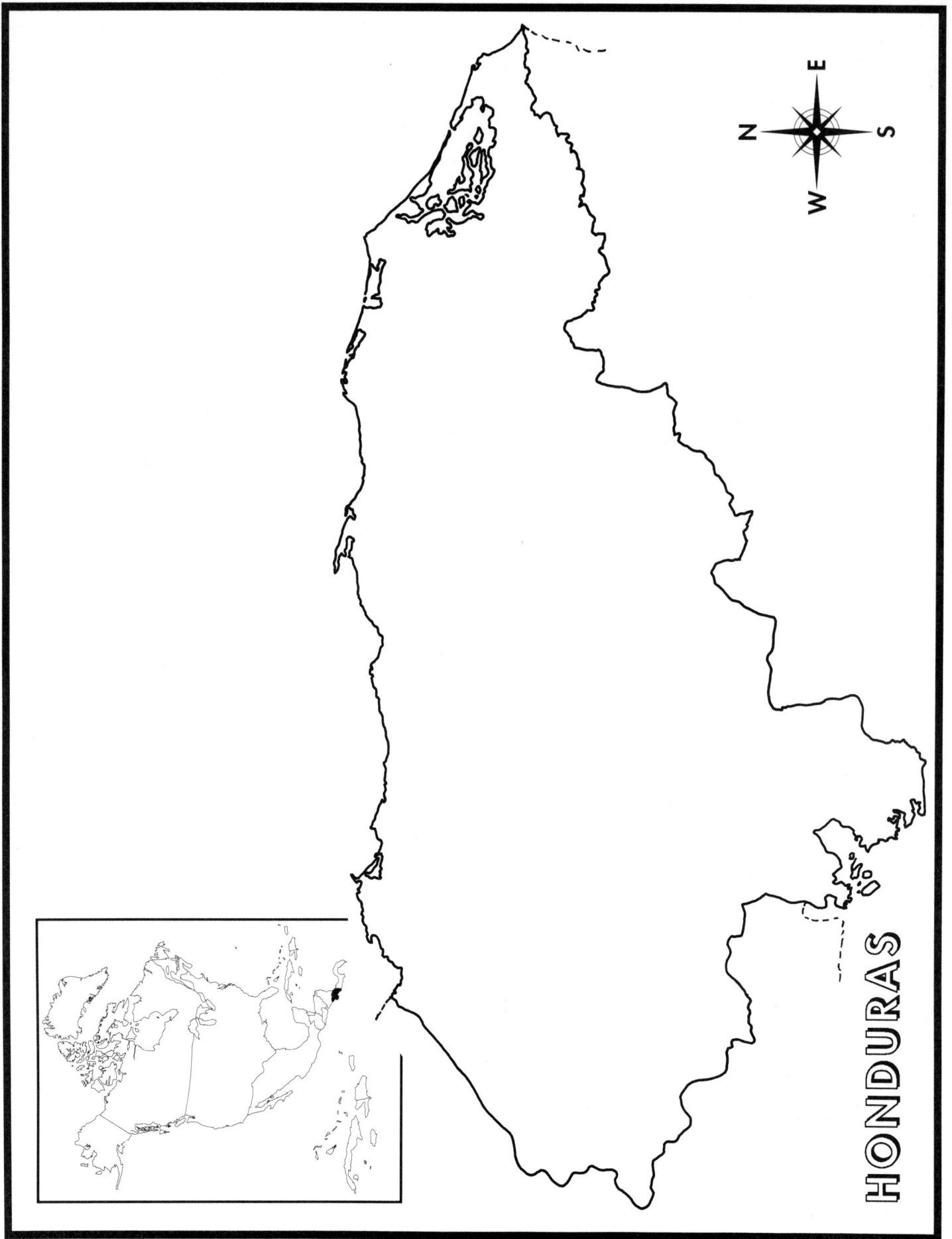

HONDURAS

HONDURAS

(hahn-DOO-ruhs)

Name _____

Date _____

DATE of INDEPENDENCE: September 15, 1821, from Spain; 1823, from Mexico. 1838, actually declared independence.

NATION'S CAPITAL CITY: Tegucigalpa.

OFFICIAL LANGUAGE: Spanish.

FORM of GOVERNMENT: Republic.

AREA: 43,277 square miles   (112,086 square kilometers).

POPULATION (est. 1989): 5,000,000 people.   _Density_: 116 people per square mile. 44 people per square kilometer. 36% urban (city) living and 64% rural (country) living.

LARGEST CITY: Tegucigalpa - 571,400 people.

ELEVATION: _Highest_: Cerros de Celaque - 9,400 feet (2,865 m) above sea level. _Lowest_: Sea level along the coasts.

ADDITIONAL INFORMATION: _Honduras_ is the Spanish word for **depths**. • It is about the size of Tennessee, and is known for the production of bananas. • Honduras is a poor country, with bananas being its main source of income. • Tegucigalpa is one of the few capitals in the world with no railroad. • About one-third of the people are **illiterate**. The country has only one University.

Honduras' Flag

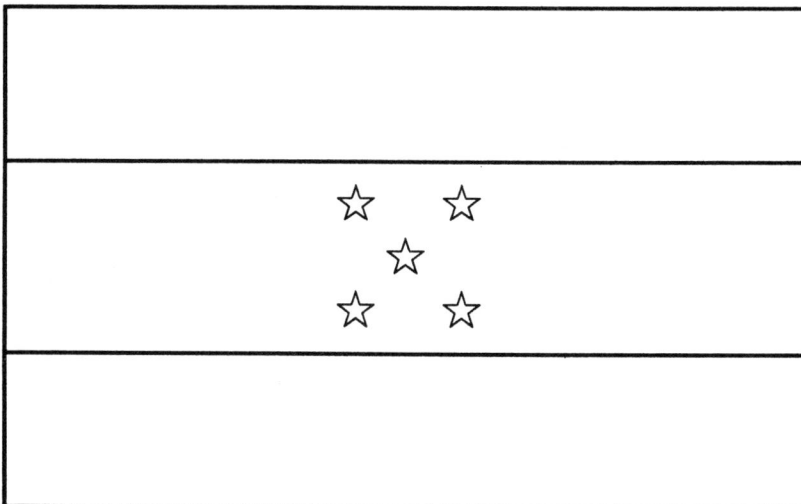

Flag Description

1. The top and bottom stripes are blue and the center stripe is white.

2. The blue stars in the white stripe symbolize the five counties that formed the United Provinces of Central America in 1823.

3. Color the flag the correct colors.

HONDURAS

(hahn-DOO-ruhs)

Name _____

Date _____

EARLY HISTORY in BRIEF

Little is known about the country of Honduras prior to the arrival of the Spanish in the early 1500's. However, it is known that an eastern center of the great Maya Indian civilization thrived at Copán until the A.D. 800's. This city of Copán had beautiful palaces, **temples** and pyramids. The Maya people were advanced in science and learning. Historians are not certain why the city lay in ruins when the first Spaniards arrived.

Christopher Columbus landed at Cabo de Honduras (Cape Honduras) in 1502. He established settlements. The Indians in the region were conquered by the Spanish settlers. Thousands of the Indians were eventually killed, died of disease or were shipped to plantations in the West Indies as slaves.

The Spanish developed gold and silver mines in Honduras. They brought thousands of black slaves from Africa to do the rugged work in the mines with the remaining Indians. Cattle ranches were also built by the Spanish settlers.

On September 15, 1821, Honduras and four other Central American states declared their independence from Spain. They became part of the Mexican empire, but broke away in 1823, to form the United Provinces of Central America. Honduras left the union and declared its independence in 1838. However, Honduras was the weakest country in Central America. (For this reason it was under the influence of its stronger neighbors, especially Guatemala.)

❏ ❏ ❏ ❏ ❏ ❏ ❏

Spanish conquistadors arrived in Honduras and helped the Spanish settlers conquer the Indians living in the region.

© GOLDEN EDUCATIONAL CENTER

HONDURAS

REVIEW QUESTIONS

Circle the correct answer.

1. Honduras became independent of Spain in ...
   - a. 1838
   - b. 1823
   - c. 1821
   - d. 1502

2. Honduras is part of ...
   - a. United Provinces of Central America
   - b. South America
   - c. North America

3. The first known white people to live in the area were the ...
   - a. British
   - b. Portuguese
   - c. Spanish
   - d. Maya

Fill in the blanks with the correct answer.

4. Today, Honduras is a _____ form of government.

5. The official language of Honduras is _____ .

6. Honduras gained its independence from _____ .

7. The capital city of Honduras is _____ .

8. The first white settlements in Honduras was started by _____ .

9. Explain what the stars on Honduras' flag symbolize.

   _____

   _____

10. Tell what happened to the Indians living in Honduras after Columbus came to the area.

    _____

    _____

    _____

11. Why do *you* suppose the Maya Indian city was in ruins when the Spanish arrived.

    _____

    _____

Mexico

MAP • FACTS • HISTORY and REVIEW QUESTIONS

New Words to Learn:

Find the words in a dictionary and write the meanings on the line.

1. **continent** - _____

2. **compose** - _____

3. **emperor** - _____

4. **isthmus** - _____

5. **magnificent** - _____

6. **sacrifice** - _____

7. **slaughter** - _____

8. **spectator** - _____

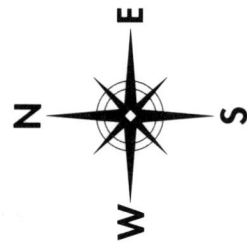

N E S W

MEXICO

© GOLDEN EDUCATIONAL CENTER

MEXICO
(MEKS-i-koh)

DATE of INDEPENDENCE: 1821, from Spain.

NATION'S CAPITAL CITY: Mexico City.

OFFICIAL LANGUAGE: Spanish.

FORM of GOVERNMENT: Republic.

AREA: The third largest country in North America.
761,600 square miles   (1,792,535 square kilometers).

POPULATION (est. 1989)**:** 86,700,000 people.   *Density*: 114 people per square mile.
48 people per square kilometer.
67% urban (city) living and 33% rural (country) living.

LARGEST CITY: Mexico City - 12,900,000 people (largest city in the Western Hemisphere.)

ELEVATION: *Highest*: Orizaba - 18,701 feet (5,700 m) above sea level.
Lowest: near Mexicali - 33 feet (10m) below sea level.

ADDITIONAL INFORMATION: Mexico is the third most populated country in the Western
Hemisphere. • In 1949, the government made an Indian the symbol of Mexican
nationality. He was Cuauhtémoc, the last Aztec emperor, whose bravery under tor-
ture by the Spanish made him a national hero. • Bullfighting is the most popular
spectator sport in Mexico. • Corn is the country's most important food.

Mexico's Flag

Flag Description

1. The left section of the flag is green
   and stands for independence. The
   middle section is white, represent-
   ing religion. The red section
   symbolizes unity.

2. Mexico's coat of arms is used
   in the middle of the flag. The
   eagle symbolizes the great Aztec
   Indian empire.

3. Color the flag the correct colors.

MEXICO

(MEKS-i-koh)

Name _____

Date _____

EARLY HISTORY in BRIEF

The first people who lived in what is now Mexico arrived in the area several thousands of years before the birth of Christ (B.C.). Historians know they were Indians. However, they do not know the particular tribes to which they belonged. It is believed that they migrated from the northern part of the **continent**. These Indians followed herds of buffalo, mammoths, and other large animals in order to hunt them for food and clothing.

By 1500 B.C., the Indians living in today's Puebla region began growing their food and became farmers. They grew corn (their most important crop), along with avocados, beans, peppers, squash, and tomatoes. These Indians were among the very first people in the entire world to grow these vegetables. Large farm villages were also developed by 1500 B.C. near Lake Texcoco and in the southern highlands. By 500 B.C., villagers began to build flat-topped pyramids with temples on them.

The Olmec Indians of the southern Gulf Coast made a major advance toward civilization in the Mexico region. They developed a counting system and calendar between 1200 B.C. and about 100 B.C. They also carved **magnificent** stone statues.

Great Indian civilizations thrived in Mexico between A.D. 300 and 900. The Maya Indians built beautiful homes, pyramids, and temples of limestone. They recorded important events on tall, carved blocks of stone and wrote in picture writing. Historians are not sure why the Maya and other great Indian civilizations declined about A.D. 900.

The fierce Toltec Indians established their empire during the 900's. Their capital was at Tula, just north of present-day Mexico City. They invaded the Yucatán Peninsula and rebuilt an old Maya religious center. They made human **sacrifices** in their religious ceremonies.

This is a picture of an old Aztec calendar.

MEXICO
(MEKS-i-koh)

Name _____

Date _____

The Aztecs built the last and greatest Indian empire the world has ever known during the 1400's. The rise of the Aztec civilization ended the Toltecs' power. The Aztec empire extended from the Pacific Ocean to the Gulf of Mexico, and from the **Isthmus of Tehuantepec** north to the Pánuco River. They were very skilled in medicine, **composed** music and wrote poetry. They were also extremely rich with gold, silver and other treasures. In Aztec religious ceremonies, they annually sacrificed their prisoners to the gods they worshipped. Their capital city of Tenochtitlán was founded in 1325, at the site of present-day Mexico City. In 1519, when the Spanish soldiers first arrived, the city had a population of about 100,000. This population was more than any other Spanish city of the time.

The Spanish began moving to the West Indies in the 1490's, and discovered Mexico in 1517. Montezuma II, the Aztec **emperor**, had heard tales of the Spanish soldiers with guns and horses (which Indians had never seen before). These tales made him fear the Spaniards as though they were gods.

The Spanish explorer Hernando (Hernán) Cortes and his soldiers totally destroyed the Aztec empire in two short years. He **slaughtered** the Aztecs for their gold and silver. In 1522, he established Spanish rule in the land and named the territory New Spain.

Spain ruled New Spain without major revolts for almost 300 years. On September 15, 1810, a priest named Miguel Hidalgo y Costilla and his followers launched the Mexican War of Independence. Three years later, in 1813, after many long and hard battles, Mexico declared its independence. However, it was not until the end of 1821, that Mexico was truly independent from Spain's control.

❏ ❏ ❏ ❏ ❏ ❏ ❏

A Mexican soldier stands ready for battle with his rifle and sabre.

MEXICO

REVIEW QUESTIONS   Date _____

Circle the correct answer.

1. Who did Montezuma II believe the Spanish soldiers were?

    a. kings   b. gods   c. explorers   d. emperors

2. In what year did the first white men probably set foot in Mexico?

    a. 1000   b. 1325   c. 1490   d. 1519

3. When did the Spanish soldiers slaughter the Aztec Indians and establish Spanish rule?

    a. 1522   b. 1519   c. 1517   d. 1490

Fill in the blanks with the correct answer.

4. The capital city of Mexico is _____ _____ . According to _____ it is also Mexico's _____ city. It is also the largest city in the _____ _____ .

5. The Indians living in the Puebla region grew _____, _____, _____, _____, _____, and _____, before they were known anywhere else in the world.

6. Why did the Spanish explorers destroy the Aztec empire? _____

7. The Olmec Indians developed a _____ & _____

8. Tell some of the advancements the Maya Indians accomplished.

_____

_____

_____

9. Tell some of the achievements, practices and skills of the Aztec Indians.

_____

_____

_____

Nicaragua

MAP • FACTS • HISTORY and REVIEW QUESTIONS

New Words to Learn:

Find the words in a dictionary and write the meanings on the line.

1. **canal** - _____

2. **economy** - _____

3. **income** - _____

4. **native** - _____

5. **neglect** - _____

6. **society** - _____

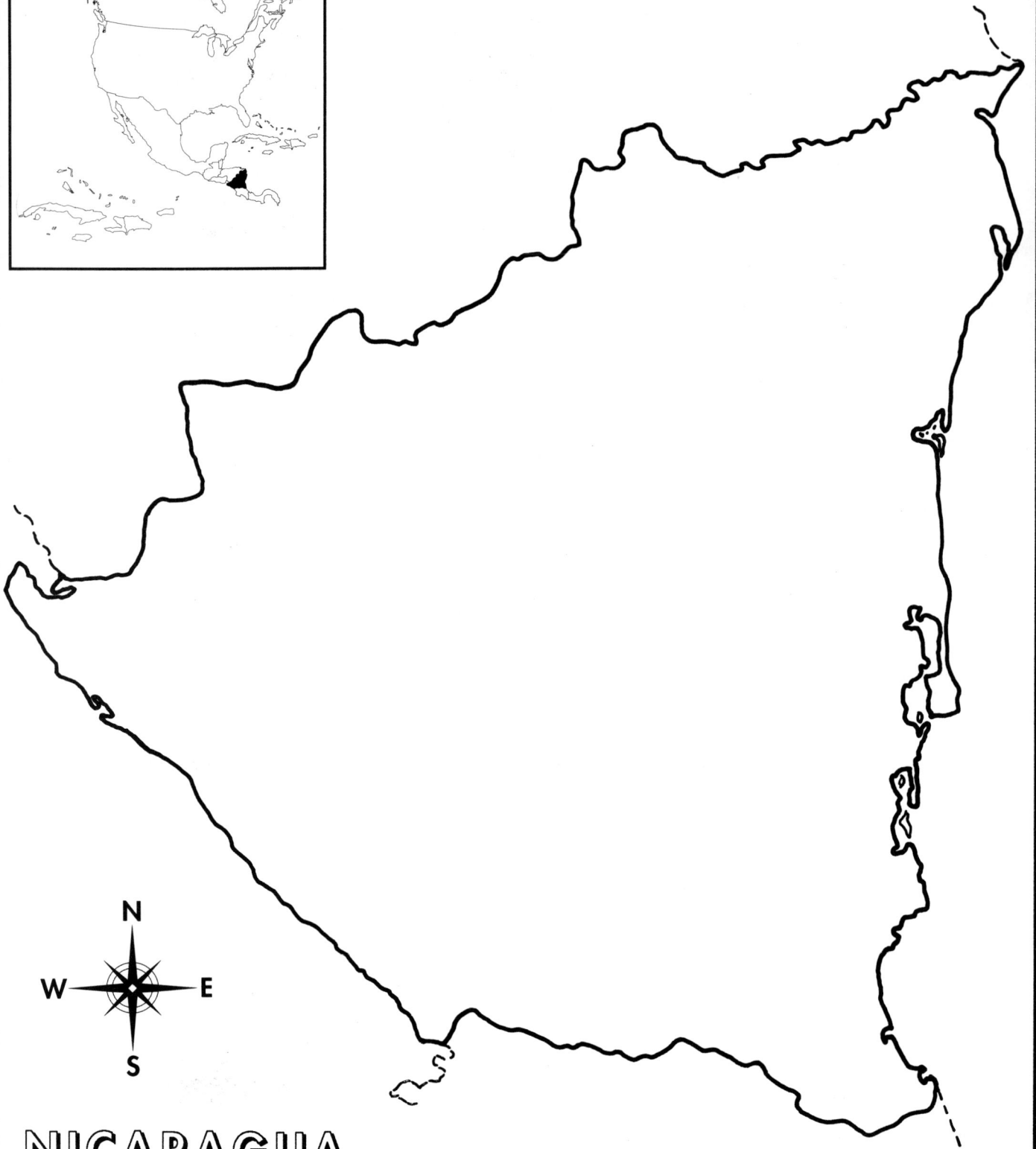

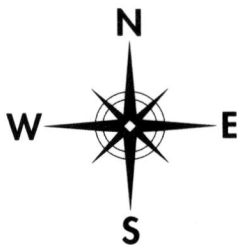

N

W   E

S

NICARAGUA

NICARAGUA
(nihk-uh-RAH-gwuh)

Name _____

Date _____

DATE of INDEPENDENCE: September 15, 1821, from Spain; 1823, from Mexico.
1838, actually declared independence.

NATION'S CAPITAL CITY: Managua.

OFFICIAL LANGUAGE: Spanish.

FORM of GOVERNMENT: Dictatorship.

AREA: 50,180 square miles   (129,966 square kilometers).

POPULATION (est. 1989): 3,500,000 people.   _Density_: 70 people per square mile.
27 people per square kilometer.
53% urban (city) living and 47% rural (country) living.

LARGEST CITY: Managua - 682,111 people.

ELEVATION: _Highest_: Cordillera Isabella - 8,000 feet (2,438 m) above sea level.
Lowest: Sea level along the coast.

ADDITIONAL INFORMATION: Most of the people of Nicaragua have both Indian and Spanish ancestors. • Cotton is the country's leading source of **income**. Most of the nation's people are poor farmers. • Only about half of the children attend school. One-third of the people over 14 years old are illiterate. • A ship **canal** was once proposed to extend across the isthmus and connect the Atlantic and Pacific Oceans.

Nicaragua's Flag

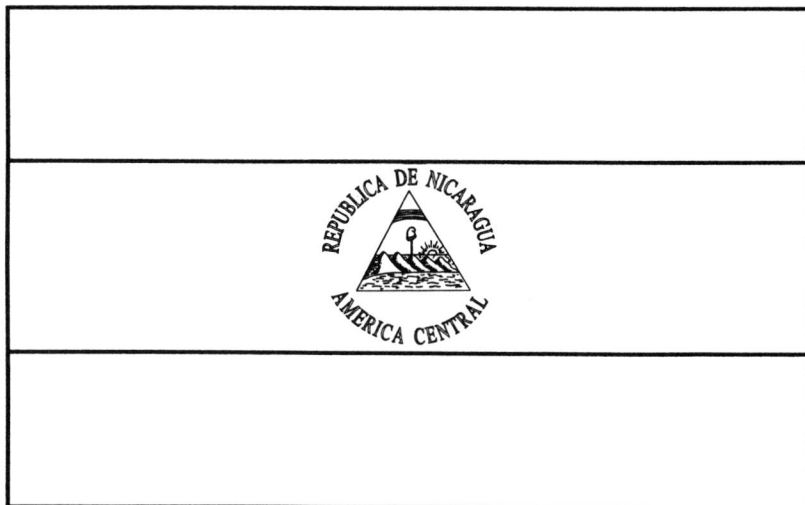

Flag Description

1. The top and bottom stripes are blue and the center stripe is white.

2. The coat of arms is in the center. The five volcanoes stand for the Central American union. The triangle represents equality; the rainbow stands for peace; and the cap symbolizes liberty.

3. Color the flag the correct colors.

NICARAGUA
(nihk-uh-RAH-gwuh)

Name _____

Date _____

EARLY HISTORY in BRIEF

Not much is known about what is today's Nicaragua before the Spanish arrived in the early 1500's. However, it is known, that a number of different Indian tribes occupied the Pacific Region and the Central Highlands. They built towns that were similar to forts. They also had markets and a social class system that included slavery. The less developed Indian **societies** in the area lived in the Caribbean Region.

In 1502, Christopher Columbus landed on the shores of what is today Nicaragua. He claimed the land for Spain. Twenty years later, a Spanish expedition from Panama explored the Pacific Region. The Spaniards converted many of the native Nicaragua Indians to the Roman Catholic religion. In 1524, another expedition from Panama came to the region and founded the settlements of Granada and León. Spanish settlers soon came to the region and used Indians to work on their farms and mines.

Nicaragua became a part of New Spain in 1570. (New Spain later became Mexico.) It was under the direct control of the *Audiencia of Guatemala* (a high court of Spanish administrators and judges.)

The Spanish explored the eastern coast of Nicaragua, but never settled in the area. During the 1600's and 1700's other people (mostly British) sometimes occupied the region. French, Dutch and English pirates had hideouts on the eastern coast of Nicaragua in order to raid Spanish ships in the Caribbean Sea. Great Britain gave up its hold on Nicaragua in the mid-1800's.

On September 15, 1821, Nicaragua, along with other Central American states, declared its independence from Spanish rule. In 1838, Nicaragua broke away from the United Provinces of Central America.

❏ ❏ ❏ ❏ ❏ ❏ ❏

Two men use grinding stones to grind corn.

© GOLDEN EDUCATIONAL CENTER

NICARAGUA

Name _____

REVIEW QUESTIONS   Date _____

Circle the correct answer.

1. Who established the first permanent white settlement in Nicaragua?
   a. Spanish   b. Portuguese   c. Columbus   d. Indians

2. What year did Columbus sight what is now Nicaragua?
   a. 1500   b. 1502   c. 1524   d. 1570

3. What year did Nicaragua break away from the United Provinces of Central America ?
   a. 1502   b. 1570   c. 1800   d. 1838

Fill in the blanks with the correct answer.

4. The capital city of Nicaragua is _____ . According to
   _____ it is also Nicaragua's _____ city.

5. In 1570, Nicaragua became a part of _____ _____ ,
   which later became the independent country of _____ .

6. _____ is the official language of Nicaragua today.

7. From what country did Nicaragua gain its independence? _____

8. Why did the pirates have hideouts on the eastern coast of Nicaragua?

   _____

   _____

   _____

9. Pretend you were a pirate with a hideout in Nicaragua. Describe your hideout and
   how you would live. (You can use extra paper if you need it.)

   _____

   _____

   _____

   _____

   _____

   _____

Panama

MAP • FACTS • HISTORY and REVIEW QUESTIONS

New Words to Learn:

Find the words in a dictionary and write the meanings on the line.

1. **encouragement** - _____

2. **holding** - _____

3. **loot** - _____

4. **voyage** - _____

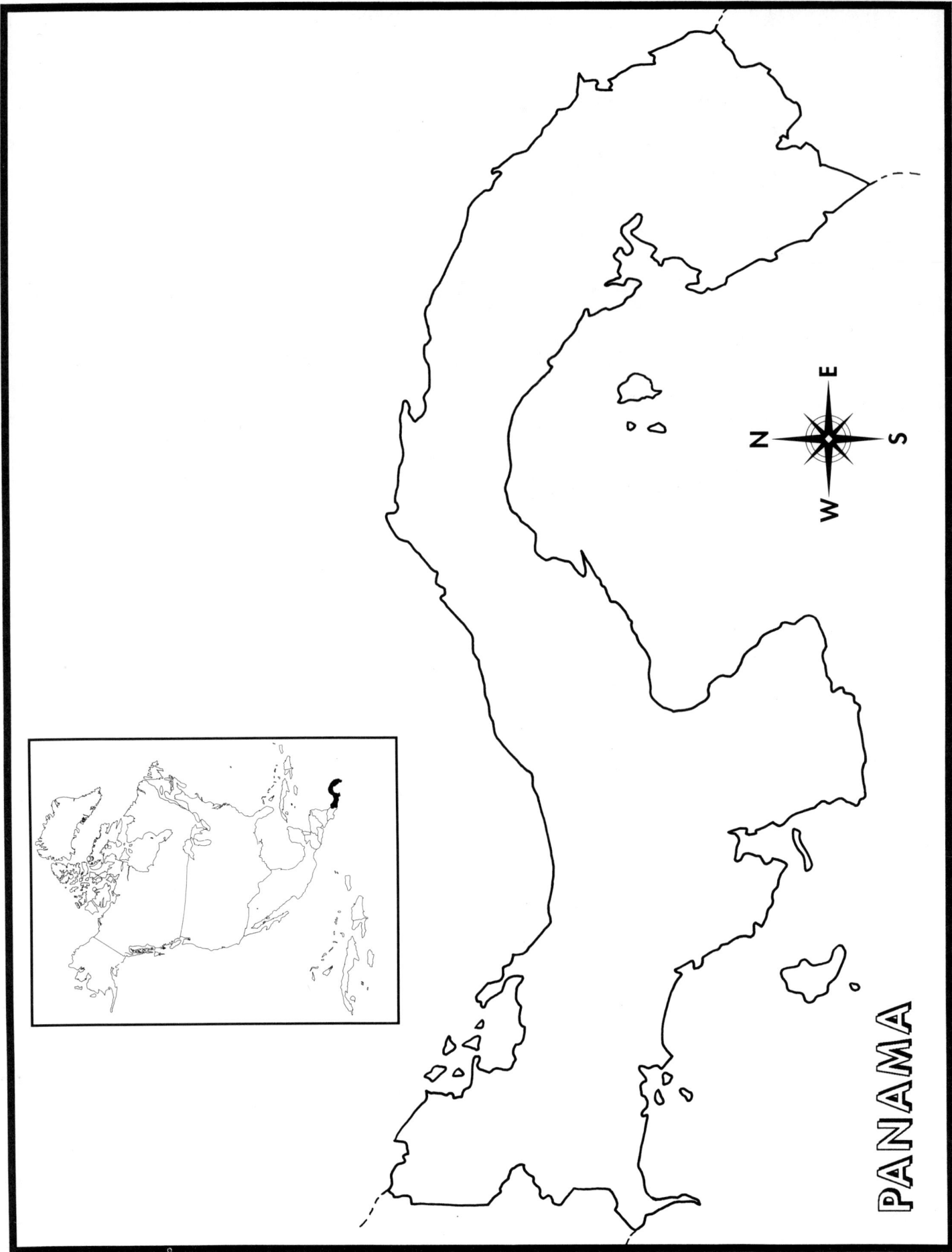

N E
W S

PANAMA

PANAMA

(PAN-uh-maw)

DATE of INDEPENDENCE: November 3, 1903, from Colombia, South America.

NATION'S CAPITAL CITY: Panama City.

OFFICIAL LANGUAGE: Spanish.

FORM of GOVERNMENT: Republic.

AREA: 29,761 square miles   (77,081 square kilometers).

POPULATION (est. 1989): 2,400,000 people.   _Density_: 81 people per square mile.
31 people per square kilometer.
51% urban (city) living and 49% rural (country) living.

LARGEST CITY: Panama City - 440,000 people.

ELEVATION: _Highest_: Volcán Barú, 11,401 feet (3,475 m) above sea level.
Lowest: Sea level along the coast.

ADDITIONAL INFORMATION: The Panama Canal is a waterway that cuts through the Isthmus of Panama. This canal links the Atlantic Ocean and the Pacific Ocean. Without the canal, ships would have to travel all the way around the southern tip of South America in order to get from one ocean to the other. In 1914, the United States built the canal over a ten year period and at a cost of $380 million. Panama is often called the _Crossroads of the World_ because of the canal.

Panama's Flag

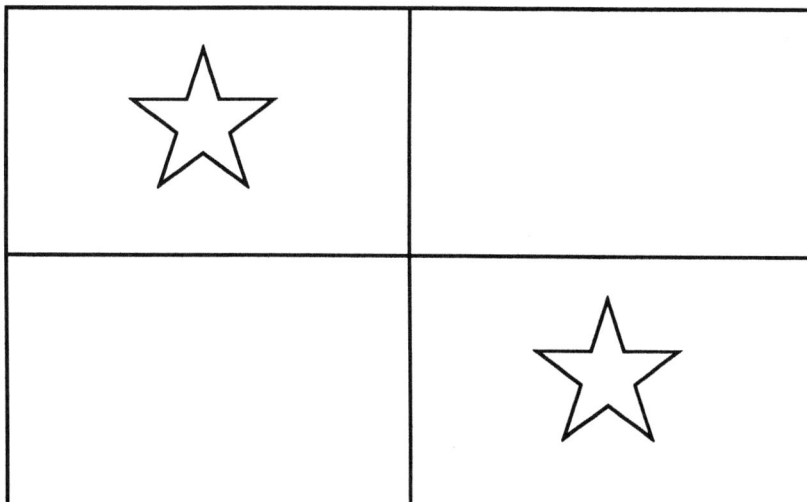

Flag Description

1. The lower left section is blue and the upper right section is red.

2. The blue star on the left symbolizes honesty and purity.

3. The right star is red and symbolizes authority and the law.

4. Color the flag the correct colors.

PANAMA
(PAN-uh-maw)

Name _____

Date _____

EARLY HISTORY in BRIEF

Indians were the first people to settle in the area known today as Panama. Historians, however, do not know when the first Indians came to the region. They do know that the Indians hunted, fished and farmed in order to live.

Just like many of the other countries in Central America, Spain conquered the Indians who were already living in the area. Spain took control of Panama in the early 1500's. The first known white person to reach the area of Panama was Rodrigo de Bastidas (a Spanish explorer). He landed in 1501. Christopher Columbus arrived in the area of Panama a year later, on his fourth **voyage** to the New World. He claimed the land for Spain. The first Spanish colonies were established along the eastern coast, starting in 1510. On September 25, 1513, the acting governor of the colonies, Vasco Núñez de Balboa, crossed the narrow Isthmus of Panama. He was the first known white person to see the eastern shore of the Pacific Ocean.

Because Panama was just a narrow strip of land separating the Atlantic and Pacific Oceans it was a very important **holding** for Spain. The Spanish destroyed the great Inca empire in Peru. The Spanish then carried the gold and other riches they had stolen from the Incas across Panama to the Atlantic Oceans in order to transport the **loot** to Spain.

The Spaniards treated the native Indians inhumanely and killed many of them. Under the Spanish, Panama became the distribution center for many of the black African slaves in the New World.

In 1819, the South American country of Colombia gained independence from Spain. Two years later, Panama broke away from Spain and became a province of Colombia. In 1830, the people of Panama staged several revolts against Colombian rule. In 1903, the government of Colombia refused to allow the United States to build the Panama Canal. With the **encouragement** and support of the United States, Panama finally became an independent nation on November 3, 1903.

❑ ❑

PANAMA

REVIEW QUESTIONS   Date _____

Circle the correct answer.

1. Who built the first permanent white settlement in Panama?
    a. Portugal   b. Spain   c. Argentina   d. Great Britain

2. What year did Vasco Núñez de Balboa cross the Isthmus of Panama?
    a. 1500   b. 1501   c. 1510   d. 1513

3. What year did Panama gain its independence?
    a. 1903   b. 1830   c. 1819   d. 1513

Fill in the blanks with the correct answer.

4. The capital city of Panama is _____ .

5. _____ landed in Panama on his fourth _____.

6. Spain used Panama as the _____ _____ for black
    African _____ in the New World.

7. _____ is the official language of Panama today.

8. _____ is the largest city in Panama.

9. From what country did Panama gain its independence? _____

10. Try to imagine that you have just been hunted and captured by complete strangers
     and taken to a completely different country. Explain your feelings, concerns and
     possibly a way you could escape. (Nobody else speaks your language.)

     _____

     _____

     _____

     _____

     _____

     _____

     _____

United States

MAP • FACTS • HISTORY
and REVIEW QUESTIONS

New Words to Learn:

Find the words in a dictionary and write the meanings on the line.

1. **adopt** - _____

2. **debt** - _____

3. **declaration** - _____

4. **inhabitant** - _____

5. **productive** - _____

6. **restrict** - _____

7. **skyscraper** - _____

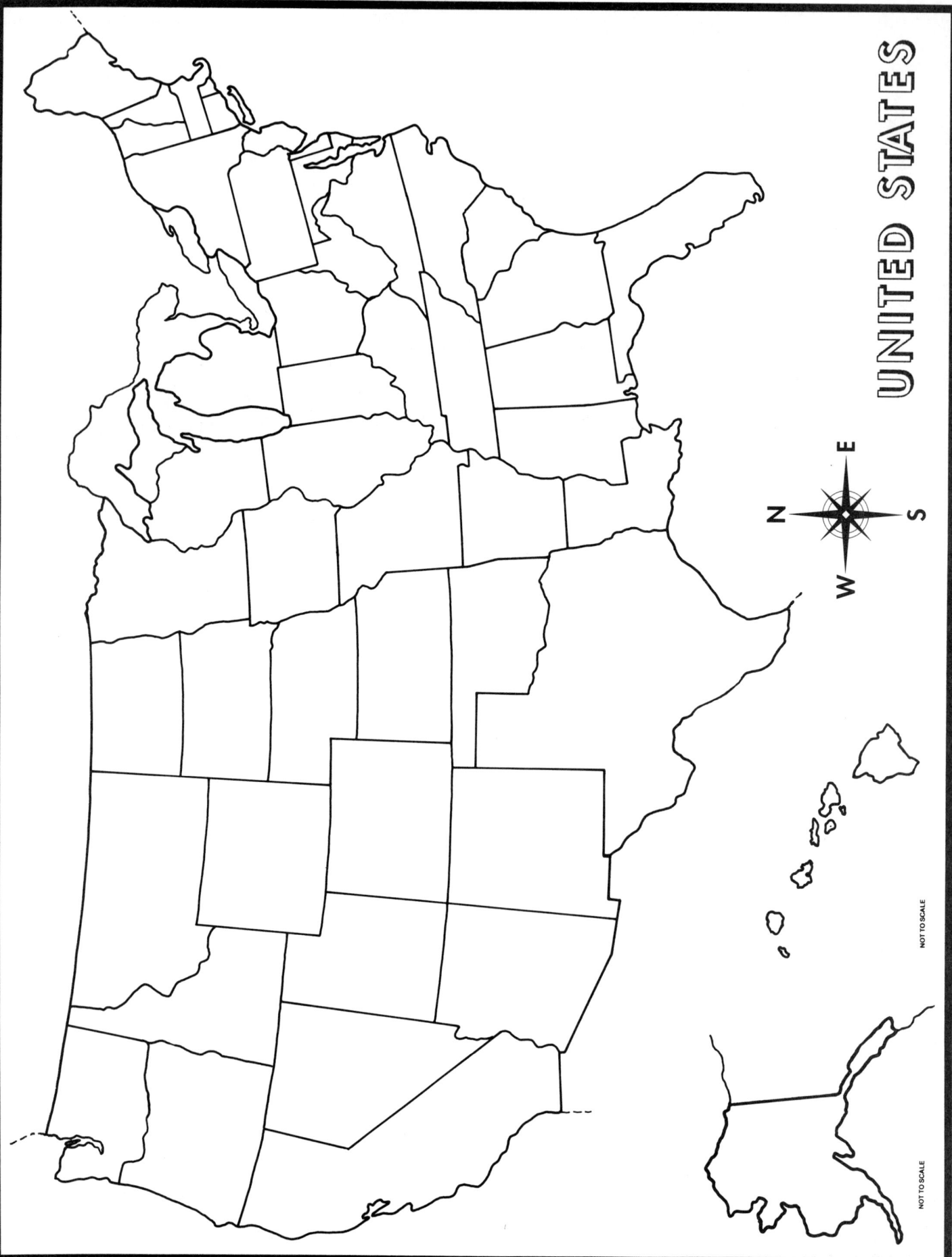

UNITED STATES

NOT TO SCALE

NOT TO SCALE

UNITED STATES
(YOO-nih-tid staytz)

DATE of INDEPENDENCE: July 4, 1776 from Great Britain.

NATION'S CAPITAL CITY: Washington, D.C. (District of Columbia).

OFFICIAL LANGUAGE: English.

FORM of GOVERNMENT: Democratic Republic.

AREA: The second largest country in North America.
3,540,939 square miles   (9,170,990 square kilometers).

POPULATION (est. 1989): 248,800,000 people.   _Density_: 70 people per square mile.
27 people per square kilometer.
74% urban (city) living and 26% rural (country) living.

LARGEST CITY: New York - 7,262,700 people.

ELEVATION: _Highest_: Mount McKinley - 20,320 feet (6,194 m) above sea level.
Lowest: Death Valley - 282 feet (86m) below sea level.

ADDITIONAL INFORMATION: The United States is the fourth largest country in the world according to population as well as area. • The population includes descendants from almost every other country in the world. • Americans developed the electric light bulb, the telephone, the steel plow, the **skyscraper** building and new art forms such as jazz and musical comedy.

United States' Flag

Flag Description

1. The stripes alternate red and white with red on the top and bottom.

2. The stars are white on a dark blue background.

3. The 13 stars represent the original colonies that became states. The 50 stars stand for the current states.

4. Color the flag the correct colors.

UNITED STATES
(YOO-nih-tid staytz)

Name _____

Date _____

EARLY HISTORY in BRIEF

Indians were the only **inhabitants** of the Western Hemisphere for several thousand years. Approximately 20 million Indians were living in the Americas when Columbus reached the New World. About one million of these Indians lived in what are now the United States and Canada. The rest of them lived between today's Mexico and the southern tip of South America.

The American Indians formed hundreds of different tribes, with almost as many languages and different ways of life. The Aztec, Inca and Maya tribes built great civilizations to the south of the United States. Most of the Indians who lived north of Mexico lived in small villages. They hunted game and grew several different kinds of foods to eat.

When the early European settlers first arrived on the continent, many Indian tribes helped them survive the wilderness. As more settlers came and moved westward, the Indians' way of life was threatened. Indians and white settlers became bitter enemies.

Before Columbus began his 1492 voyage from Spain, Europeans did not know the Western Hemisphere existed. Columbus, as well as other European explorers, were searching for a short sea route to the Far Eastern countries of India and China.

On October 12, 1492, Columbus landed on the Caribbean island of San Salvador. The island is located east of the North American Mainland. Europeans called the land he had reached the *New World.* They also named the entire Western Hemishpere *America*, after Amerigo Vespucci. Amerigo was an Italian explorer who sailed to the New World for Spain and Portugal in 1497.

To many Europeans, the New World offered opportunities for wealth, power, adventure and freedoms not known in Europe.

This native American Eskimo is making a hunting tool out of bone.

UNITED STATES
(YOO-nih-tid staytz)

During the 1500's, Spain and Portugal explored the southern part of the Western Hemisphere while the British and French concentrated in the northern regions. The Spanish quickly destroyed the Inca Indians of Peru, the Mayans of Central America and the Aztecs of Mexico. Portugal took control of what is now Brazil. Spain also moved into what is now the Southeastern and Western United States. They controlled Florida and the land west of the Mississippi River. They founded St. Augustine, Florida, in 1565, the oldest city in what is now the United States.

The French settled mostly in the area that is now Canada. The British settlements were mainly in what became the United States (including the 13 colonies that later became the United States.) France and Britain fought for many years for control of the land between the Atlantic Ocean and the Mississippi River, as well as Canada.

In 1607, about 100 British colonists founded the first British settlement in North America. It was near Chesapeake Bay, Maryland. They named the colony, *Jamestown*. They suffered great hardships from cold winters and many died from disease. However, the settlers managed to survive and build **productive** farms.

In the 1600's, as the colonies grew, enslavement of black Africans began. Slavery flourished in the South, where large plantations grew cotton, tobacco and other crops. By 1860, there were about 4 million slaves in the United States, about one-third of the South's population. The inhumane practice of slavery was abolished after the Civil War in 1865.

By the mid-1700's, most of the settlements had been formed into 13 colonies. They stretched southward from Maine to Georgia. The colonies included New Hampshire, Massachusetts, Connecticut, Rhode Island, New York, New Jersey, Pennsylvania, Delaware, Maryland, Virginia, North and South Carolina, and Georgia. (Maine was part of Mass.)

After the French and Indian War, Britain wanted to strengthen its control over its American colonies. It also had a huge national **debt** from war expenses. The British government started taxing the the American colonists as well as **restricting** their freedoms. Many conflicts took place, and finally, on July 4, 1776, the colonies declared their independence and formed the United States of America by **adopting** the **Declaration** of **Independence**. In 1883, seven years after the Revolutionary War had started, the British were finally defeated. ❑ ❑ ❑ ❑ ❑ ❑ ❑ ❑ ❑ ❑ ❑ ❑ ❑ ❑ ❑

UNITED STATES

Name _____

REVIEW QUESTIONS

Date _____

Circle the correct answer.

1. From what country did the United States gain its independence?
   a. Spain   b. the Netherlands   c. Great Britain   d. France

2. The official language of the United States is ...
   a. Spanish   b. Dutch   c. English   d. French

3. About how many Indians were living in the United States when Columbus arrived?
   a. None   b. hundreds   c. one million   d. twenty million

Fill in the blanks with the correct answer.

4. What date did the United States declared its independence? _____

5. The United States is the _____ largest _____ in North America.

6. How many years passed from declaring war until the British were actually defeated in the Revolutionary War? _____

7. The American Indians were made up of _____ of different tribes.

8. Actually, Columbus, did not realize the _____ _____ even existed. He thought he had landed in _____ . That is why he called the people living in the area "Indians."

9. Both North and South America were named after the _____ explorer, _____ _____ .

10. List and memorize (Yes, memorize!) the 13 colonies that became the original 13 states.

_____

_____

_____

_____

_____ Have your teacher or a friend test you on the states you have just memorized!

North America

Answer Keys

NORTH AMERICA

REVIEW ANSWERS

Section 1 - Bahamas (page 5)

1. c. 1717
2. a. 1492
3. c. bases for trading ships
4. Britain
5. Nassau
6. Spain
7. enslaved; gold mines; Hispaniola
8. never
9. English
10. 1973
11. Abolished
12. *Teacher check*

Section 2 - Belize (page 11)

1. English
2. d. British Honduras
3. d. 1981
4. Maya; Yucatan Peninsula; 1500-300 A.D.
5. Captaincy General of Guatemala
6. British; shipwrecked; settlement; 1638
7. Constitutional Monarchy
8. Belize City
9. Spain; Guatemala; Territory
10. *Teacher check*

Section 3 - Canada (page 18)

1. Toronto
2. Canada; New Brunswick; Nova Scotia; Ontario
3. French; English
4. Iceland; first; 1000 A.D.
5. 1931
6. *Teacher Check*
7. *Teacher Check*
8. *Teacher check*
9. New France; Province of Quebec; Dominion of Canada Kingdom of Canada (optional)

Section 4 - Costa Rica (page 23)

1. c. 1000
2. b. Spanish
3. c. Republic
4. San José; population; largest
5. Christopher Columbus
6. permanent; Cartago
7. Mexican
8. enslave; Indians; fought
9. 1838
10. Spain
11. *Teacher check*

NORTH AMERICA

REVIEW ANSWERS

Section 5 - Cuba (page 29)

1. a. Spain
2. d. Spanish
3. c. West Indies
4. 1902
5. sugar; tobacco; enslaved; died; disease; harsh
6. Christopher Columbus
7. United States
8. hanged them
9. *Teacher check*
10. *Teacher check*

Section 6 - Dominican Republic (page 35)

1. b. Spanish
2. b. East
3. c. West Indies
4. first voyage
5. oldest; Hemisphere; University of Santo Domingo
6. oldest; Western
7. Santo Domingo
8. Caribbean Sea
9. *Teacher check*
10. *Teacher check*

Section 7 - El Salvador (page 41)

1. c. 300
2. a. 1524
3. d. 4524
4. 1841
5. Spain
6. western; cities; crops; weavers
7. Democratic Republic
8. San Salvador
9. *Teacher check*

Section 8 - Guatemala (page 47)

1. Republic (Dictatorship)
2. Spanish
3. September 15,1821 (1839 declared)
4. Guatemala City; population
5. *Teacher check*
6. *Teacher check*

NORTH AMERICA

REVIEW ANSWERS

Section 9 - Haiti (page 52)
1. a. France
2. b. 1788
3. d. Columbus
4. Dictatorship
5. Western
6. France; January 1, 1804
7. *Teacher Check*
8. *Teacher Check*
9. *Teacher check*

Section 10 - Honduras (page 59)
1. c. 1821
2. c. North America
3. c. Spanish
4. Republic
5. Spanish
6. Spain
7. Tegucigalpa
8. Christopher Columbus
9. The five countries of the United Provinces of Central America
10. *Teacher check*
11. *Teacher check*

Section 11 - Mexico (page 66)
1. b. gods
2. d. 1519
3. a. 1522
4. Mexico City; population; largest; Western Hemisphere
5. corn; avocadoes; beans; squashes; peppers; tomatoes
6. gold and silver
7. counting system; calendar
8. *Teacher check*
9. *Teacher check*

Section 12 - Nicaragua (page 69)
1. a. Spainish
2. b. 1502
3. d. 1838
4. Managua; population; largest
5. New Spain; Mexico
6. Spanish
7. Spain
8. to raid Spanish ships in the Carribbean Sea
9. *Teacher check*

NORTH AMERICA

REVIEW ANSWERS

Section 13 - Panama (page 77)

1. b. Spain
2. 1513
3. 1903
4. Panama City
5. Christopher Columbus; voyage
6. distribution center; slaves
7. Spanish
8. Panama City
9. Colombia
10. *Teacher check*

Special Notes & Doodles

_____
_____
_____

Section 14 - United States (page 84)

1. c. Great Britain
2. c. English
3. c. one million
4. July 4, 1776
5. second; country
6. 7 years
7. hundreds
8. Western Hemisphere; India
9. Italian; Amerigo Vespucci
10. New Hampshire, Virginia, Massachusetts, Connecticut, Rhode Island, New York, New Jersey, Pennsylvania, North and South Carolina,Delaware, Maryland, and Georgia. (Any order is correct.)

_____
_____
_____
_____
_____
_____
_____
_____
_____
_____
_____
_____

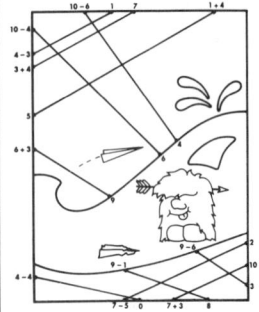